The Radiant Life

The Radiant Life

Truman G. Madsen

BOOKCRAFT
Salt Lake City, Utah

Library of Congress Catalog Card Number: 94-72408
ISBN 0-88494-938-9

2nd Printing, 1995

Printed in the United States of America

CONTENTS

PUBLISHER'S
FOREWORD

Truman G. Madsen brings a blend of unique talents and perspectives to his work. Although recognized internationally for his scholarship and impressive academic credentials, he is perhaps best known for his ability to teach in a way that reaches the heart. Because his fervent testimony and deep feelings for the Savior and the gospel undergird his teaching, his words carry tremendous emotional power, stirring those same feelings and emotions in the inner lives of those who hear him.

He has made the study of the life of the Savior and His modern-day prophet, Joseph Smith, a lifelong commitment. His study has led him to publish a number of books and tapes, and their impact has been felt both in and beyond the Church. He has a remarkable ability to explain profound truths in terms all can understand and to convey a sense of the interrelationship of gospel principles.

All of these abilities and experiences are brought to bear in the chapters of this book, which brings together in one place not only transcripts of outstanding recordings but also stimulating writings, both published and unpublished, that represent some of the best of the author's work. Brother Madsen addresses a wide range of subjects with the skill, conviction, and clarity that have become his hallmarks. He treats vital principles such as prayer, love, faith, and forgiveness in powerful and touching ways, drawing upon his abilities as a storyteller and his grasp of the history of ideas to highlight and inspire. Again and again, he focuses on the Savior—how we can come to *know* Him (not just know *about* Him) and have our lives illuminated by His light. The book teaches eloquently how we can worship with the whole soul and experience the fulness of joy the gospel has to offer.

Bookcraft is honored to offer this thought-provoking, timeless work that will help strengthen the faith and deepen the commitment of all who read it.

1

SOULS
AFLAME

There is a legend about a grandfather, a holy man, who, caring for his grandson, sent him out to play. Shortly the boy returned, sobbing as if his heart would break. He explained: "I have been playing hide-and-seek with my friends. I went and hid and waited, but no one came for me." The grandfather embraced him and said: "Now you know how God feels. He hides, and no one comes for Him."

This church does not have a collection of what in classical terms is called devotional literature, nor again an official manual, which is a set of spiritual exercises. What we do have is a pool of experience, rich experience. Here I would like to select from it some bits and pieces that I believe will draw us closer to them and, through them, to the Lord.

There are religions in the world which in effect develop prayer practices after the preconceptions of their theology are taken into account. We have an opposite heritage. Our theology has been derived from prayer—this is safer, sounder, and saner, I believe. But first may I mention two hard reflective hang-ups that occur in the discussion of prayer and that have not only been resolved but also dissolved for us if we only will accept this.

First is the notion that God, being all-powerful and all-knowing, is therefore unchanging. And that since He knows all that will occur—having, it is said, absolute foreknowledge—prayer is pointless. For if God knew yesterday what is happening today, including all that I am going to do, then it is pointless to ask that it be changed. Though one can insist that His foreknowledge is not a cause, one can still ask, "But am I a cause, truly, if in fact the eventuations could not have been otherwise?"

The heritage of prayer in this church teaches us that, whether or not we settle the question of foreknowledge, there is point in reaching up to that personage who is himself free and has used His freedom to forbid to himself the use of force. He is not a computer, not a thing, I am grateful to report. He is a conscious being, and it is the relationship of our freedom to His freedom that does make a difference.

Our history is filled with instances in which what seemed to be inevitable was prevented from happening by the intervention of our prayers and God's response.

A second cause of confusion is the notion that God, being God, must know what is best for us; and that therefore if we pray and ask Him to change His mind, He would hardly be wise to answer yes. If we pray to our own hurt, a loving God would do well to answer no. And if we are simply praying to remind Him of what He already intends, why pray at all? There is a kind of intellectual lockjaw that comes from such reflection, but in truth again, the Restoration makes it clear that we have a need and that so does He, and that He needs us to listen as well as to ask. It is said among the Jews that, God preferring prayer to mere silence and not receiving it, caused great affliction among the Israelites of the Exodus, so they would at least cry out from their pain.

We do need Him and He does need us, and one would almost gather from diaries and journals which report firsthand experience that His will can be swayed—in part because the very prayer process changes us, and God can respond to the change; and in part because, in the two-way relationship that exists, we learn and grow through His response.

I turn now to questions that are more soulful and reply with experience. There is, some insist, a circularity in faith itself. Faith, the child once said in a Sunday School class, "means believing what you know darn well isn't so." Faith is sometimes thought to be in the religious world a substitute for reason, and in fact a form of credulity. It is thought to be faith that something is or isn't. But the first principle of the gospel of Jesus Christ is not such faith. It is faith in a person about whom we already have some knowledge. Faith is not exerted in vacuo. Trust in a person is based upon acquaintance with the person, or at least belief about the person that begins secondhand. But the whole point of the gospel is to make it firsthand. So He who counsels us, "Pray always," is asking that we come to Him in confidence.

Second, it is said that prayer is a crutch. After all, mature people are supposed to stand on their own two feet; they don't have to pray. Prayer is a form of wishful thinking, a kind of wanting pie in the sky. Well, as to that, first of all there is nothing wrong with crutches for people who need them. There is nothing wrong with escalators and elevators. But speaking of crutches, agnosticism is a kind of crutch. It is a perennial postponement of decision, and it assumes that postponement is safer than commitment. Atheism is a pair of iron braces. It claims to know more than can be known. Someone has said that atheists don't find God for the same reason that bank robbers don't find policemen. They work very hard to avoid Him. But throughout the Doctrine and Covenants is the admonition, "Seek and ye shall find." The implication is, don't seek and you likely won't find.

But it is said: "I don't pray because I have doubts. I doubt things about myself, about the gospel, and even about God." It is truly said that doubt and faith do not coexist in the same person at the same time, but they can exist within a second of each other. Witness Heber C. Kimball's standing by the door while Brigham Young was lying on what appeared to be his deathbed. Said Heber, "I doubt very much if Brigham ever rises from that bed."

However, "he had no sooner uttered the words, than he spoke up, as with another voice, and said, 'He *shall* live, and shall start upon this mission with me tomorrow morning.' And they did start the very next morning, on their mission to England." (Orson F. Whitney, *Life of Heber C. Kimball* [Salt Lake City: Bookcraft, 1967], p. 434.) He was right the second time. From doubt to faith.

On another occasion he stood in the Bowery in Salt Lake City and announced to threadbare and barely surviving people. "States goods will soon sell in Salt Lake City for less than they sell for in New York. In the name of the Lord. Amen." And as he returned to his seat from the pulpit, he said he "had missed it this time." Someone on the stand said, "I don't believe a word of it." And Brigham Young said, "Let it stand." It did stand. When the

California gold rush came, the prophecy was actually and completely fulfilled. Elder Kimball was right the first time and he went from faith to doubt. (See *Life of Heber C. Kimball*, pp. 389–90.)

It is an honest prayer to say: "Lord, I believe. Help thou mine unbelief." And it was, after all, a prophet of God, Joseph Smith, who said—and he was a man of faith—"If I had not experienced what I have, I could not have believed it myself" (*Teachings of the Prophet Joseph Smith*, comp. Joseph Fielding Smith [Salt Lake City: Deseret Book Co., 1976], p. 361).

But it is said: "I don't pray because I am not good with words. I would rather someone else would do the talking." Fair enough, but our history is filled with instances of people who had mind-boggling verbal gifts and of others who did not. There have been many, like Moses, who needed an Aaron. And there are in our midst today those who are both deaf and dumb, whose lips are sealed but who yet may pray from their core wordlessly. Joseph Smith offered a better rendering of the King James Version's line by Paul that says "the Spirit maketh intercession for us with groanings which cannot be uttered" (Romans 8:26). The Prophet's version is "with striving which cannot be expressed"—meaning, in words (see *Teachings*, p. 278). But if a person does have trust in the living God, he can from his core reach upward, put an arrow on those imprisoned needs, and they will be carried by the Spirit, perfectly communicated and responded to. And what relief when we do it!

But it is said, "I do not pray because my prayers have not been answered." Answered, we mean, do we, not heard? Ah, but they have been heard and recorded. We are taught that one day we will have a perfect, bright recollection of all that has been in our lives here, but what of all that has been before that? The historian B.H. Roberts thought long and hard on the record, and he pursued this subject so often and so deeply, trying to account for the radical differences he perceived among those who have received the gospel in this dispensation. Seeing that some seemed almost to be born with it, and had responses to the gospel and its powers far beyond anything they could have learned in the short space of mortality, he concluded that they did bring it with them. Thus his summary was "Faith is trust in what the spirit learned eons ago." We do come here bringing, though they are locked under amnesia, the residual powers, the distillation of a long experience. And to those of us who see the hand of the Lord everywhere and to those who see it nowhere the same promise is made: The day will come when we shall know that we have seen Him, and that He is the light that is in us, without which we could not abound (see D&C 88:50). There is locked in all of us as there was in Enos—and I understand Enos to say he was surprised that it was there—more faith than we presently know. We are heard, but the response of God may not be what we would here and now wish. Yet haven't we lived long enough to say to the Lord, "Disregard previous memo," to thank him that He answered no, and to ask that He erase some of the requests that we now realize were foolish or hasty or even perverse?

Now may I take slices from autobiographical accounts. Are we to pray in practical terms or specific terms? It is said that on one occasion Brigham Young, hung up on a sand bar crossing a river on the plains, had a companion who said, "Let's pray." To which Brigham is supposed to have replied: "Pray? I prayed this morning. Let's get out and push." There is a time for total concentration in prayer and a time for answering prayer with one's own muscles and initiative.

This is the same man who was specific enough to bring to the Lord concrete and urgent feelings, even hostile ones. It is said he left his prize saddle once, in the proper place, but someone misplaced it or didn't hang it properly and the horse trampled it into shreds. He rebuked the man who had shown the neglect, and then made a beeline for the bedroom, where he said (someone overheard him), "Down, Brigham!" Then he knelt and said: "Lord, I am sorry. I was angry. Take my anger away and help me to do better next time." "When I am angry," said a friend of his, "the first thing I do is pray." Some of us have been taught that should be the last thing we do, that we should soak our head in a bucket and then pray. "I am never so angry but what I can pray," said Heber C. Kimball. (*Journal of Discourses* 3:231.) The same goes for related emotions.

In the same spirit, Brigham Young once said: "I do not recollect that I have seen five minutes since I was baptized that I have not been ready to preach a funeral sermon, lay hands on the sick, or pray in private or in public." Think of that. Then he added: "I will tell you the secret of this. . . . If you commit an overt act, repent of that immediately and call upon God to . . . give you the light of His Spirit." (*Journal of Discourses* 12:103.) Why spend a week rationalizing and defending what you have done amiss or have not done aright?

Can we pray when there is really hardly the heart for it? Lorenzo Snow leaves us the glimpse that after he was, as he felt, stillborn into the Church, nothing really significant happened in and after his baptism and confirmation. He kept praying for the witness of the Spirit. It didn't come. Not only not feeling as he was wont, but feeling that the heavens were as brass over him, he nevertheless went to an accustomed place to pray. He had no sooner opened his lips than the Spirit descended upon him in a marvelous way. He described it as like the sound of rustling silken robes—they did not have the word *electricity* then. This experience was more tangible in its effect upon every part of his body than being surrounded by water in baptism. He was filled, though praying when he didn't want to pray. (See *Juvenile Instructor* 22:22.)

But are we not to bring a certain proper reverence to prayer, and if we are out of that, should we not repent and wait? Listen to Heber C. Kimball. He is praying with his family and in the midst of the prayer says, "Father, bless Brother So-and-So." Then he bursts into a loud laugh. I can imagine the heads of his children popping up and their eyes opening. There is a slight pause, and then he says, "Lord, it makes me laugh to pray about some people," and he goes on with his prayer. (See *Life of Heber C. Kimball,* p. 427.) I leave you to say whether that is lightmindedness or profound intimacy with the Lord. He knows. We have a funny bone. He gave it to us.

My father taught me this ancient legend about Adam and Eve. As they were departing from the garden, there was a solemn farewell, the Father recognizing far more clearly than they did what they, as vanguard pioneers in the real world, were going to face. They said good-bye, but just before the couple disappeared in the mist the Father couldn't stand it. He called them back and gave them a sense of humor.

We are admonished not to betray the sacred. That is lightmindedness. "Remember that that which cometh from above is sacred, and must be spoken with care, and by constraint of the Spirit; and in this there is no condemnation, and ye receive the Spirit through prayer; wherefore, without this there remaineth condemnation" (D&C 63:64).

But we are also blessed that we should have a glad heart and a cheerful countenance. If you cannot laugh at yourself and even at some of the absurdities of this world, you take yourself too seriously. Prayer can manifest that phase of one's core with divine approval.

But again, there is the problem of method. Do you have to say it a certain way? Do you have to have an appropriate technique? We may say: "I don't know whether I am sincere or not. I don't know whether I want to pray or not." In the right circumstances this is an acceptable prayer.

But can you cry out of affliction with any hope of help? Of course. It was Joseph Smith in the dungeon at Liberty Jail who asked the questions we all sooner or later will: "O God, where art thou?" And the second question, "How long O Lord?" To the first question, the answer was, "I am here," and to the second, "Not long, but a small moment, Joseph." Note that it was the Lord's definition of time. "If thou endure it well and art faithful, thou shalt triumph." (See D&C 121:1–2, 7–8.) I am impressed with the number of miracles of overcoming, of solving problems, but I give it as my testimony that equally impressive are those divine blessings that enabled people to endure what they could not overcome, to hold on, to wait and wait and wait.

But can one pray for the impossible? There is in certain traditions about omnipotence the inferential notion that one could ask that a friend who had been killed in a foreign war the day before should yet live. That God, having command of time, could actually answer the prayer with yes. Not so, I submit. There are laws. There are conditions. And God himself cannot change them. "Yes," we cry out, "He could and sometimes does prevent this or that." But He could not prevent it and still accomplish other of his multiple purposes. It must be rough to be the Father of everyone.

Is there a name that we are most often to use, which He prefers? Good question. It is answered in the life of Christ, who chose almost without exception one word—Abba. In Hebrew it means "Father," but it means a shade more than that. It means as a child would whisper it, "Daddy." Intimate. We are all given names after we are born, and the Lord wills to give us a name after we are reborn. We take it upon us, willingly and by covenant. It is His name. And through it and with it we are equipped to pray more powerfully than if we prayed only in our own name. In my imagination, I wonder if when the personage said, "Joseph, this is my beloved," He might also have said, "Beloved, this is our Joseph." Or, if it might have been that they stood in visitation—which is more than vision, and must have been bewildering at least at the outset—and could have said, "Remember us?" We are to use the name of Him who descended below all things.

From the above slices I come to a focus and a conclusion. There are levels beyond levels of prayer. There are heights beyond heights. There are promises in modern revelation that in due time, after we have proved that we are determined to serve the Lord at all hazards, then we may receive keys whereby we may ask with the assurance of an answer.

Said Joseph Smith to Brigham Young on an occasion, "You have passed certain bounds and conditions, Brother Brigham," and Brigham explains, "he passed certain bounds before certain revelations were given" (*Manuscript History of Brigham Young* 4:19). Brigham passed the same keys to others, including Wilford Woodruff. Wilford Woodruff is the one who said at the dedication of the Salt Lake Temple that it had been made known to him by revelation that the reason a representative of the Woodruff family had been called to preside was that "the Lord could not find a weaker vessel" (Salt Lake Temple Dedication Notes, April 1893, p. 125, in Church Historical Department).

Our whole history teaches that out of weakness we can be made strong. Why does the Lord choose the weak? Among other reasons, it is because they can be taught and influenced, whereas He has to use a jackhammer on the proud. Further, because they are transparently weak, those who have eyes to see are not confused on where the power really comes from.

There are levels beyond levels, gifts beyond gifts. I summarize them with this glimpse. It was in a school of instruction, the school of prophets—and prophetesses, too. The first thing the Smith brothers thought on a day of rich spiritual outpouring in that room above the Newell K. Whitney store was, "Where is mother?" They sent a messenger in great haste, who brought her to participate. (See *History of Joseph Smith by His Mother* [Salt Lake City: Bookcraft, 1956], p. 224.)

In such a setting the Prophet asked that each in turn speak; that, as the revelation says, all might not speak at once, but that everyone might have an equal privilege (see D&C 88:122). The subject was faith. Scriptures were quoted. The last man to speak, as it happened, was Heber C. Kimball, who told of an experience in his own family. His daughter, Helen Mar, was standing by a table on which dishes were stacked. Her mother warned the child as she left the house: "Stay away from those dishes. If you break one of them I will whip you." Vilate left, and Helen Mar did what little children do when they are told not to do it. To her dismay, she let a table leaf fall, and several dishes were broken. What now? She went out, as she had watched her parents do, and near a tree she prayed that her mother's heart would be softened. We don't know just what she said, but no doubt it was simple enough, such as, "Bless my mother that she won't whip me." When her mother returned, she saw the situation. She flared. She took the girl by the hand into the bedroom, intending to administer the promised punishment. But she couldn't do it. We can imagine the scene—the arms of her daughter around her neck and the child saying, "Oh, Mother, I prayed that you wouldn't. I'm sorry, I'm sorry."

When Brother Heber had finished telling the story, every man in the room, including Joseph, was in tears. And Joseph said—to those grown-up, strong, independent, willful, intelligent men—"Brethren, that is the kind of faith we need. The faith of a little child going in humility to its parent." (See *Life of Heber C. Kimball,* p. 69.) That sums it up.

This verse is a fitting conclusion: "Pray always and I will pour out my Spirit upon you, and great shall be your blessing—yea, even more than if you should obtain treasures of earth and corruptibleness to the extent thereof. Behold, canst thou read this without rejoicing and lifting up thy heart for gladness? Or canst thou run about longer as a blind guide? Or canst thou be humble and meek, and conduct thyself wisely before me? Yea, come unto me thy Savior." (D&C 19:38–41.)

2

IN A PLACE
CALLED GETHSEMANE

A prophecy uttered by the Prophet Joseph Smith in 1841 is in fact being fulfilled before our very eyes "Jerusalem must be rebuilt and the temple, and water come out from under the temple, and the waters of the Dead Sea be healed" (*Teachings*, p. 286), and all this before the coming of the Son of Man. When my wife, Ann, and I first touched that ground with our feet I had a prejudice that the setting of the Savior's life really was not significant; the meaning of His words was what mattered, and the environment and circumstances of the time were not crucial. After many visits since, for we have both visited and lived there, I am of the contrary opinion. I believe that He cared very much about the setting, and that meaning is lodged still in the very rocks, in the very mountains, in the very trees of Israel.

On many of our trips to Israel we had groups mostly of persons we would consider young, but on one trip there was a woman past eighty-two, who had to prepare for it at length—had to exercise and get constant reassurances from her physician as to whether she could endure the rigors. We were touched that as we walked away from a church that has been built near (and some say over) the ancient site of Gethsemane, she who had come so far and lived so long was on her knees near the place where tradition says Jesus knelt.

North of Jerusalem is the Galilee. And in visiting there I am struck that the location of Caesarea Philippi is at the mount called

Hermon. Some possibility assigns it as the Mount of Transfiguration, but it is in any case at the headwaters of the Jordan, which then feed the Galilee and then flow south and are literally the nourishment of all Israel. It was there, and I think Jesus chose the place carefully, that He announced to Peter, after Peter's confession, that He would build His church as on a rock. I think it is significant that there is there still a huge faced rock, and below it and in it a cave; and out of that cave, at the time Jesus stood there, there flowed water. Not so since—an earthquake changed all that. But was Jesus therefore saying to Peter, whom He knew by revelation was to be His presiding Apostle, and of Peter, who by revelation had recognized Him, "Upon this flowing rock I will build my church"? (Matthew 16:18.) Well, such are the suggestions of the setting. Is it also, one may ask, only happenstance that He chose to be baptized near the waters called dead at the lowest point of the earth—1200 feet below sea level—descending thus even physically below all things?

There are trees in Israel, and we are taught from the record that each in a way was significant in the Savior's ministry: palm trees, fig trees, oak trees, but most of all olive trees. Even to this day the process of planting, cultivating, pruning, and harvesting from olive trees is a laborious one. And the process of then taking the olives, which at first are bitter and useless, and going through another step of hard labor and pressure to produce ripe, mellow olive oil—that too is done today. In the time of the Master olives and olive oil and the olive mash that resulted from the crushing were the very essence of life. All that comes clearly to mind as one stands there.

Religious literature is permeated with the notion that a tree of life is representative of eternal life. It is planted in a goodly land, some traditions say on the very navel of the earth, the highest point of the earth; which, symbolically at least, is the temple mount in Jerusalem. A tree planted and watered by the waters of life whose fruit is the most precious. Our own Book of Mormon says further of that fruit that it is sweet, that it is pure, even that it is white (see 1 Nephi 8:11; 11:8). And there are even now, incidentally, in Hebron, in Israel, magnificent vineyards where the very fruit itself is white, almost transparent. These happen to be the sweetest and the purest of the grapes. The imagery that it was so precious impressed Nephi after he was given the blessing of recapitulating the vision of his own father, Lehi. And he said it when asked—yes, precious, I beheld precious. But ever that superlative didn't satisfy the angel, the narrator of the vision who said, "Yea, and the most joyous to the soul." (See 1 Nephi 11:9, 23.)

Well, the tree of life has been utilized through sacred history as the symbol both of Israel and of the Redeemer of Israel. And there are traditions that in due time that tree, from which the branches had been broken off and dispersed, would somehow be planted anew, and graftings and gatherings take place anew, until the tree was again productive.

The olive tree is not deciduous. Its leaves never fall off. They are rejuvenated and stay. It is in that sense evergreen or ever olive-colored. It is a wild thing if not cultivated. But after long and patient cultivation, usually eight to ten years, it becomes productive; more than that, it continues to be with age. And there are trees today—for new shoots come forth from apparently dead roots—that are known by actual horticultural study to be eighteen hundred years old. Some trees on the Mount of Olives may be older than that. One could almost say of the olive tree, "It is immortal."

Olive oil is used by many today in the Middle East as a condiment for salads or as a cooking oil. But in the Savior's day olive oil was the very substance of light and heat in Israel. An olive lamp, into which one poured the pure oil and then lighted it at one end, provided light even in a darkened room, enough light to fill the room. Moreover, the mash provided fuel and burned long. And the balming influence, the soothing, salving influence of olive oil, was well known in the Middle East. The tradition of the balm of Gilead and the soothing even of troubled waters was well known in Jesus' own day.

We speak today of the olive branch as a symbol of peace and forgiveness. Paul even refers to "the oil of gladness" (Hebrews 1:9). It is in that sense also symbolic of joy.

Did Jesus know all this? Surely He did. Was there then something significant in His choice of the mount known as the Mount of Olives? And was it true then, as now, that Mount Oilvet was symbolic and sacred, all of it? Let me remind you that on that mount four holinesses came together in a remarkable way. I speak first of the place. It was eastward from the temple, a temple which by now had been desecrated, the temple which He first called on a day of cleansing "my Father's house," but which later He spoke of as "my house." (John 2:16; Mark 11:17.) In that house was a Holy of Holies. Two olivewood pillars stood as entrances, and they were in fact connected to the menorah, the perpetual lamp, and from them came two kinds of tubes, into which were poured olive oil; then it burned.

A Jewish tradition says that when Adam, close to the time of his own death, was debilitated, he sent Eve and his son Seth back to the garden for the healing oil. But at the threshold they were met by an angel who said there would be no oil again until the meridian of time when the Messiah would come, and then the oil would be that of the olive tree.

Another tradition, based on a scripture in Leviticus, says Moses was commanded to teach the children of Israel to bring to him for the tabernacle olive oil, "pure olive oil beaten for the light" (Leviticus 24:2). The tradition says that such oil was burning in the time of Jesus; but it had lost its sacred significance, or had not yet received its sacred fulfillment.

Jesus went on the mount overlooking the temple mount, as, says the scripture, "he was wont" (Luke 22:39). Luke even says that in the last days of His life He lodged there, He "abode there" at night (see Luke 21:37). On that hill was a garden, but the more proper word is vineyard. A vineyard of olive trees? Yes. That same word is used in the parable or allegory of the tame and wild olive tree as related in the book of Jacob. The Lord of the vineyard, Dr. Sidney B. Sperry believed, was the Father of us all. The servant in the vineyard was the Messiah. His task, the weightiest in all history.

It is called Gethsemane. *Geth* or *gat* means "press," and *shemen* in Hebrew means "oil." The place of the olive press. You can see such presses still in Israel, for after the processes of salt and vinegar and pressure came the time when they gathered the olives, placed them in a bag, and then with a huge crushing rock (to push it usually required an animal) they crushed those olives until the oil flowed. The place of the olive press.

Another holiness was the week of Pesach, Passover. Ann and I have been privileged to attend that still kept and honored, sacrosanct celebration—Passover. Since the destruction of the temple it has been modified. At the time of Jesus they brought the lamb, the faultless lamb (and, by the way, down that very mount), to the altar, and it was slain and the blood sprinkled on the altar. That was the season—the time.

As for the person, this was Yeshua Massiach, Jesus the Messiah, a stem of Jesse, so Isaiah prophesied, from the stump or the root of the house of David (see Isaiah 11:1). He who had been the Revealer to Abraham, Isaac, and Jacob. He who had not only approached but sat upon Jacob's well, and to a despised woman announced, for the first time on record: "I am He. I am He from whom shall flow living waters." (See John 4:14, 26.) It was He who had been prophesied. The word *messiah*, as it appears today in the King James Version in Daniel 9:25–26, has roots of "the anointed one." Now came the night when He would become the anointing one.

Further, the word *messias*, as it is used in the Gospel of John, has another root: *tsahar*, meaning to glow with light as one glistens when one is anointed. To earn the name, the holiness of the name, He had to tread the press. That image is used by Isaiah, but the Lord himself uses it in our own time, in that remarkable summation revelation the Prophet Joseph gave us of that glorious vision recorded in Section 76 of the Doctrine and Covenants. "I have trodden the press" (in this case the wine-press, but the two merge). "I have . . . trodden the wine-press alone, even the wine-press of the fierceness of the wrath of Almighty God" (D&C 76:107).

Having spoken of the holy place, the holy time, the holy person, and the holy name, may I offer a glimpse of what must have gone through Him and of what He must have gone through. "Mine hour," He had said often, "has not yet come," but now it had. After the Last Supper the record says, "and it was night" (John 13:30). Thus an explanation—I think we need no other—for why the three Apostles couldn't stay awake even though He pleaded.

Somewhere, somewhere on that mountain, He knelt.

I have witnessed the effort of the most pious of Jews as they stand—they do not kneel—at the place that is but a remnant of the wall below the ancient walls of the temple mount. Rhythmically, they throw their whole bodies into their prayer. They are sometimes ridiculed for this. They say: "We are fighting distraction. We want to concentrate. Movement helps." Well, the movement of that night, I suggest, was internal, not external, and somehow the bitterness was as bitter as gall. Not just the family of our Father who dwell upon this earth were affected, but, as we have been taught by the Prophet Joseph Smith, those of other earths also (see Bruce R. McConkie, *Mormon Doctrine,* 2d ed. [Salt Lake City: Bookcraft, 1966], pp. 65–66). So the atonement of Jesus Christ is intergalactic in its effect. That burden, that bitterness, He vicariously took within. "How?" we cry out. But a child can understand. Pain hurts. Even the presence of it hurts those of us who merely stand detached and observe. The Savior, who is supersensitive and did not take a backward step from the will of the Father, could and did feel for and with us. The pressure worked upon Him. Somewhere on the road between the north and the south, He cried out, anticipating, "Father, save me from this hour." We don't know how long was the interim between that sentence and prayer and the next, but He then cried: "but for this cause came I unto this hour. Father, glorify thy name." And the voice said, "I have both glorified it, and will glorify it again." (John 12:27–28.)

Luke, who tradition says was a physician, recorded that great drops of blood came from the Savior's pores (Luke 22:44). The bitterness oozed. It is not a spectacle one wishes to recall, but we have been commanded, and weekly we memorialize it in an ordinance called the sacrament. Even then, all His preparation and all that He could summon from His own strength was not sufficient. And more earnestly, says the record, He prayed, and an angel came, strengthening Him (see Luke 22:43–44). Strengthening, but not delivering. What is it like to have the power to summon legions of angels to end the ordeal yet not to summon them? During that same night He was betrayed. He was taken prisoner. He was broken into, pierced by scourging; and a merciful reading of Pilate's motives suggests that he hoped this would suffice for those who were crying out against Jesus. It did not. The weight, I submit, had begun there on the mount, a much greater weight than the weight of the cross that He was then to bear.

Now, what conclusions can we draw from all this? First, hereafter when we speak or hear the words, "I anoint you with this consecrated oil," let us remember what the consecration cost.

As we sit—but in our spirits as we kneel during the sacrament service—and are asked to remember His body, recall that it was the veritable tree and olive beaten for the light, and that there flows from that mount unto this whole earth, and beyond, the redemptive power of healing and soothing and ministering to the needy.

In the hours of gladness, should our cup run o'er, let us remember that to make that possible a cup—the bitterest of cups—must have been drunk.

On that day when our life, the life of attempted faithfulness, is bludgeoned and becomes wearing and wearying, may we remember that no great and good fruits come easily, that we are the olive plants who were supposedly planted anew in Him, and that only time and suffering and endurance can produce the peaceable fruit which He yearns for us to have. He does not deliver until the perfect work has done its work.

Finally as we go into the days of affliction which have on every level and through all the prophets been promised us, hard days, let us remember that from that mount, in what most would have thought was the most tragic event of history, has come the source and power of purification and life. One day He will honor it again, this time descending in His glory. And when His foot touches it, this whole earth will know it. The mount itself shall separate, be shaken, and an earthquake will follow. The earth itself will be purged and cleansed and will eventually shine with celestial light. We are promised we may be there, either to descend with Him or to ascend to meet Him, and either of those is glorious. Over and over He spoke of himself as the bridegroom preparing His own for a feast. In our own Doctrine and Covenants we have been promised that feast, when all worthies who have been made worthy will gather (see 58:3–11). In the beginning of this dispensation, this revelation was given: "Wherefore, be faithful, praying always, having your lamps trimmed [that means full] and burning [that means alight and afire] and oil with you, that you may be ready at the coming of the Bridegroom" (D&C 33:17).

I bear witness that Jesus is the Messiah and that He could not have known, according to the flesh, how to succor His people according to their infirmities unless He had gone through in Gethsemane what He went through. I bear testimony that the knowledge He has today, what one of the prophets calls "the bowels of mercy," reaches out unto the Father, who grieves that any tree in His vineyard should be lost. He pleads even now for more time, for you and for me, until we too have been purged and can sing the song of redeeming love.

3

MAN
ILLUMINED

The sum of this chapter can be put in one word: *Light*. We see with and through light; but we rarely examine light itself. Yet continually why and what and how questions are put to me which, I am convinced, are less questions than they are questings, questings for Light.

No theme is more central to modern revelation than light "which lighteth every man that cometh into the world" (John 1:9). The Church itself came "out of obscurity and darkness" into the light, and the light of modern revelation centers in Christ. Consider the following excerpts:

> That which is of God is light (D&C 50:24).
>
> That which doth not edify [lift, inspire, enliven] is not of God, and is darkness (D&C 50:23).
>
> He that ascended up on high, as also he descended below all things, in that he comprehended all things, that he might be in all and through all things, the light of truth (D&C 88:6).
>
> And the light which shineth, which giveth you light, is through him who enlighteneth your eyes, which is the same light that quickeneth your understandings (D&C 88:11).
>
> Truth embraceth truth; virtue loveth virtue; light cleaveth unto light [as darkness cleaveth unto darkness] (D&C 88:40).
>
> Light and truth forsake [detect and withdraw from] that evil one (D&C 93:37).

[Christ's light] is *in* all things, giveth life to all things ["maketh alive all things" (Moses 6:61)] . . . is through all things [surrounds, envelops, permeates] . . . is the law by which all things are governed. (D&C 88:13, 41.)

And if your eye be single [constantly upreaching and out-reaching] to my glory, your whole bodies shall be filled with light, and there shall be no darkness in you; and that body which is filled with light comprehendeth all things (D&C 88:67).

Then shall ye know that ye have seen me [Christ (indirectly in the light of sun, moon, and stars, but directly in a former condition of glory in his presence)], that I am, and that I am the true light that is in you, and that you are in me; otherwise ye could not abound [that is, live, grow, flourish] (D&C 88:50).

Every man whose spirit receiveth not the light is under condemnation. For man is spirit. (D&C 93:32–33.)

That which was from the beginning is plainly manifest unto them, and they receive not the light (D&C 93:31).

He that keepeth his commandments receiveth truth and light, until he is glorified in truth and knoweth all things. (D&C 93:28.)

He that receiveth light, and continueth in God, receiveth more light; and that light groweth brighter and brighter until the perfect day [the day of perfect light, the light of the perfect day] (D&C 50:24).

From these revelatory and sweeping insights into the nature of light and the light of nature, one senses the beginnings of the whole cosmology, a prodigious and unifying key to the secrets of the vast universe. I select only those themes that apply to man himself, his makeup, his comprehension, his life fulfillment.

Light as the Real

These revelations suggest that man is more than a receptacle of degrees of light; he is somehow in his very primal makeup composed of light. One associate of the Prophet Joseph Smith understood him to say "that light or spirit, and matter, are the two great primary principles of the universe, or of Being; that they are self-existent, co-existent, indestructible and eternal and from these two elements, both our spirits and our bodies were formulated."

It is implicit in this statement that "pure light" (if that means unembodied light) is somehow less advanced than the living light that comes in the complex organization of spirit bodies and physical bodies—could we say "light magnified"?

Yet the Prophet added: "Light and heat . . . fill the immensity of space, and permeate with latent life, and heat, every particle of which all works are composed." (Letter from Benjamin F. Johnson to George Gibbs, p. 7, in Church Historical Department.)

Light and heat are, even in their grosser forms, refining and welding influences. But the light and heat in the fusion of realities that is man transcend somehow the lesser and grosser forms of light.

Light as Truth

If, then, light is interfused with man's spirit and physical bodies, we may see how fitting it is to say that light is truth. The glorified Christ says, "I *am* the Truth." Elsewhere He speaks of himself as "the Spirit of Truth" and in the same vein "the light of truth." And again as "Intelligence, or the light of truth," and says, "I am more intelligent than they all" (Abraham 3:19), more intelligent, that is, than all other intelligences.

Truth in one sense is, as our hymn says, "the sum of existence." It is another name for reality, that which is. But in a second sense, "truth is knowledge" (D&C 93:24), the accurate perception of that which is. Christ himself has become the truth in both senses. First, He is the fulness of personality: He is the sum of human existence. Second, He illumines the truth for us. By experiencing the struggle toward perfection, He "descended below all things" into darkness that "comprehended him not" (D&C 88:6; 45:7). Thus He received a fulness of the glory of the Father, which is a fulness of the light of God. And having made that light His own, He is for us the source of "the life and the light, the spirit and the power, sent forth by the will of the Father" (D&C 50:27).

In mortality the more light one receives, the more he can receive. We grow and glow not just by addition but by multiplication. Hence the promise, "For unto him that receiveth it shall be given more abundantly, even power" (D&C 71:6), and its correlative warning, "But whosoever continueth not to receive, from him shall be taken away even that he hath." (JST Matthew 13:11.)

The more a person increases in light, the more he gains access to truth and acquires intelligent consciousness of all that light penetrates—on the one hand the immensity of space and, on the other hand the immensity of time, "things as they are, and as they were, and as they are to come" (D&C 93:24). Eventually he may receive the fulness of light that circumscribes all truth.

Said Brigham Young:

> It is not the optic nerve alone that gives the knowledge of surrounding objects to the mind, but it is that which God has placed in man—a system of intelligence that attracts knowledge, as light cleaves to light, intelligence to intelligence, and truth to truth. It is this which lays in man a proper foundation for all education. (*Discourses of Brigham Young,* comp. John A. Widtsoe [Salt Lake City: Deseret Book Co., 1946], p. 257.)

When we are told, "If ye receive not the Spirit ye shall not teach" (D&C 42:14), it means more than that we should not. We cannot. More—without it, we cannot even understand. "Why is it," the Lord asks, "that ye cannot understand and know, that he that receiveth the word by the Spirit of truth receiveth it as it is preached by the Spirit of truth? Wherefore, he that preacheth and he that receiveth, understand one another, and both are edified and rejoice together." (D&C 50:21–22.) Teaching any truth, even the most elemental or simple facts, is exciting to both teacher and student. Touched by the light, they tend to see the infusion, the "hand of God," as it were, everywhere.

> And I have felt
> A presence that disturbs me with the joy
> Of elevated thoughts; a sense sublime
> Of something far more deeply interfused.
> (Wordsworth, "Lines written a few miles above Tintern Abbey.")

But one who has yet to respond needs what the Prophet once referred to as a rebirth of one's eyes or a change of heart before he can see any difference between the kingdom of God and the kingdom of the world (see Andrew F. Ehat and Lyndon W. Cook, eds., *The Words of Joseph Smith* [Provo: BYU Religious Studies Center, 1980], p. 256). Such a one moves about unaware of any light. Just as 20-20 vision is helpless without light, so, in the wider world of the spirit, the "eyes of the understanding" must be quickened.

Quickened carries at least three strands of meaning—"to enliven, to hasten, to permeate." Careful introspection will show that there is no mental process that is not intensified by the subtle enlightening process described by the Prophet—"when you feel pure intelligence flowing into you" (*Teachings*, p. 151). Not only are there "sudden strokes of ideas," the "first intimations," but also a brightening effect that enables us to see what we saw before, but now in quite literally a new light. The effects extend to the person as a whole—even his balance, coordination, and motor skills. In the understanding, light has to do with the clarifying of concepts and judgments (more than analytic proficiency), with the heightening of imagination (more than aimless fantasy), with the recovery and interweaving of memories (more than chance deliverances of the subconscious), and with the strivings and inspirings of creativity. These phenomena take a person beyond the "light barriers." His mental life is "brighter."

The teaching that our "whole bodies" can be full of light (D&C 88:67) suggests that what we call I.Q. is a clumsy and misleading "measure" of man's cognitive powers. Genuine intelligence, or the conscious "light of truth," is the light that recognizes and absorbs or "cleaves" to truth, and it involves the whole person. Intelligence, in short, is a kind of light-susceptibility. Hence the Prophet needed a Urim and Thummim until he himself became one. We have a glimpse of that level of light and burning in the Prophet as he emerged with Sidney Rigdon from his chamber, after they had written "while yet in the Spirit" a portion of what they had together beheld in the vision of the degrees of glory (D&C 76). His statement is: "My whole body was full of light and I could see even out at the ends of my fingers and toes" (N.B. Lundwall, comp., *The Vision* [Salt Lake City: Bookcraft, n.d.], p. 11).

We are reaching toward this awareness when we say, "I know with every fiber of my being. . . ." The scriptures are replete with testimony that the capacities, the hidden potential, the lava of our inner responses to truth far exceed any plaudits ever offered for the "genius." We can no more "drink up the ocean" than we can learn all truth "line by line." But "that body which is filled with light comprehendeth all things" (D&C 88:67), and the ocean, indeed all oceans, are subject to the rays that proceed from and return to Him who is "glorified in truth" (D&C 93:28) and "knoweth all things" (D&C 38:2).

The principle "truth embraceth truth; virtue loveth virtue; light cleaveth unto light" (D&C 88:40) helps us explain many of the experiences of the religious struggle. For example:

—How five minutes is sufficient to bring vibrant and total trust for one person, and fifty years not long enough for another, though the "evidence" or record is the same for both.

—How the most intense sympathy, empathy, and social feelings emerge in settings of light and spiritual experience, a mutual kinship out of mutual kindling.

—How enslaving habits and degenerate compulsions in the flesh, which stand like an impenetrable shield between the spirit of man and the Spirit of God, can be purged and purified—burned out—by a light-power that heals and redeems. And why the statement "you can't change human nature" is simply *false* if "you" includes your spirit and Christ's Spirit power.

—How light can be glaring and unpleasant, even blinding, when first we are subjected to it, but then the increasing intensities and heats become more than endurable; they render our former condition repugnant.

—How grosser light stops with surfaces and casts shadows, but the higher light can be in us and through us.

—How we "receive the Spirit through prayer" (D&C 63:64), but also we need to improve our prayer pattern until we pray with the Spirit and "in the Spirit" (D&C 46:28–30).

—How there are two kinds of burning in us; one a burning of conscience, urging and lifting us to become what we have in us to become (and accumulating guilt in postponement), and second a burning of approval and peace when we set about repenting.

—How negative feelings can restrain the peace and power of light as it flows down, yet the flow of the Spirit can melt away all such dross if we will permit our spirits to take the lead.

Light as the Good

If light is somehow the substratum of all reality and also of all intelligent awareness of reality, it is only another step to say that light is the foundation of good. In few, if any, ancient or modern cultures has "light" become symbolic of evil, "dark" of good. Instead, light tends to be identified with the good, the valuable, the blessed, the sacred. But it is more than a symbol or a ritual. The scriptures teach that the light of Christ is given to every man that comes into the world, but that it enlightens "through the world" all those that hearken (D&C 84:46). Light edifies, lifts, and "that which does not edify is not of God and is darkness" (D&C 50:23). That is the bound and condition of all law, physical and moral, the "law by which all things are governed" (D&C 88:13). Light is not just the test of good; it is the nature of all that is judged truly good. Alma, who in earlier years had emerged from guilt-ridden darkness that made his own extinction seem desirable, wrote, "Whatsoever is light is good, because it is discernible" (Alma 32:35).

In the realm of the good, as elsewhere, light is the "bound and condition" of all preferred ways of life. And these bounds and conditions are inexorable and exceptionless, not because they tell us what our choices must be but because they tell us what the *results* of our choices will be. Of course, one can attempt to "become a law unto [himself]" (D&C 88:35), but only at the cost of diminishing the light. Every minute of every day we are increasing or decreasing in our receptivity to light, and there is no way to escape the inevitability of that consequence in our thoughts, our acts, our very breath. One can look upon the law of light either as the enemy of freedom or as freedom's guarantee, which "is preserved by law and sanctified by the same" (D&C 88:34). One can abide the law only as one can abide the light, and vice versa.

An unconditional imperative can be derived from this: Seek the increase of Christ's light. And all commandments are instrumental to this end, which is an intrinsic value. If it is said (as it is fashionable to say) that such an imperative is only binding upon me if I make it so, that if I find it unappealing, or meaningless, or even absurd, then it is not mine and therefore is not binding at all, one reply is that a measure of light itself is essential even to such a denial of the light. Christ is the true light that is in us, even when we turn our backs on Him. He himself became God by abiding in the light. And even God is bound by the law.

Light as Beauty

From the understanding that light is the root of reality, of truth, and of goodness, the next step is to recognize that light is the foundation of beauty. And, again, not only does light enhance the beautiful—light itself is beautiful.

The scriptures, and notably the Book of Mormon, teem with Hebraic symbols for the beautiful and the lovely, revolving around light, brightness, fire, and whiteness. Thus of the vision of the tree of life that Lehi and Nephi beheld, it is written: "The beauty thereof was far beyond, yea, exceeding of all beauty, and the whiteness thereof did exceed the whiteness of the driven snow" (1 Nephi 11:8).

Similarly one can feel the ancient writers straining for superlatives in their descriptions of white fruit, "to exceed all the whiteness that I had ever seen" (1 Nephi 8:11), of white robes or clothing, "nothing upon earth so white" (3 Nephi 19:25), and of the white virgin, "exceedingly fair and white . . . most beautiful and fair above all other virgins" (1 Nephi 11:13–15).

Artists have often depicted this recognition of light as divine beauty by the halo, the nimbus, and the golden circle above the head. But that is at best a token of the promise and the actuality. For "whole bodies" are promised illumination, and the light not only hovers over but also surrounds and engulfs the entire personality until it is gloriously beautiful. It was, after all, every one of the multitude, and all of each of them, even the seams of their clothing, that became scintillant with white light in the presence of Christ during that "ineffable outpouring of prayer," as Elder James E. Talmage calls it, in the 3 Nephi narrative (see 3 Nephi 19:25). Modern men and women of God who have witnessed such radiance of soul say it is "like a search light turned on within." It is "the same glorious spirit," the Prophet once wrote, "gives them the likeness of glory and bloom. . . . No man can describe it to you—no man can write it." (*Teachings*, p. 368).

Aesthetic delight, then, whatever else it is, is delight in light. And it is surely significant that the whole color spectrum, every vivid color of the rainbow, harmonizes in white light which, in turn, harmonizes in Christ.

At the everyday level there are the light-variations in the human face, almost infinitely intimate and animated. "You will always discover in the first glance of a man, in the outlines of his features, something of his mind," said the Prophet Joseph (*Teachings*, p. 299). Particularly around the eyes ("the light of the body is the eye" [Matthew 6:22]), the forehead, and the lips one sees recorded a person's past and present encounters with light. It has nothing to do with fairness of complexion, with age, with cosmetic skill, with habitual patterns of facial set or mood, or even with the features we are accustomed to identify as "attractive." One must remember Isaiah's telling—should we say warning?—prophecy of the Messiah: "there is no beauty that we should desire him" (Isaiah 53:2). Later Christ could see through the rough and rugged exterior of John the Baptist and call him "a burning and a shining light" (John 5:35). And John the Beloved could say of Christ that "in him is no darkness at all" (1 John 1:5). The true beauty "in the eye of the beholder" is also in the eye of the beheld, and the glory of both. It is the divine light of beauty, as also the beauty of divine enlightenment, and it comes from above before it comes from within. Not all who are handsome or beautiful in the conventional sense are illumined. But all who are illumined, though conventionally "plain" or even "ugly," are beautiful.

The face may also reflect darkness. It is no abuse of terms to say that in some faces, and in all of ours at times, there is an "aura of darkness" that is disagreeable and unbeautiful, encircling in its gloom. *Darkness* here is not just a metaphor for attitude. It is an apparent absence of light that prefers and reflects "works of darkness" and finds the presence of light too much. No artifice successfully conceals it, not even a perpetual and mannerly smile. Seeking to become appealing, which is the ultimate testimony that light is good and beautiful, the adversary himself "transformeth himself nigh unto an angel of light" (2 Nephi 9:9). But his is "dark light"; and as the Master warned us, "If therefore the light that is in thee be darkness, how great is that darkness!" (Matthew 6:23.) Having fallen from a condition of brilliant light, having flouted the inner light, Satan and those he seals his own in "outer darkness" are in deliberate darkness that cleaves to and surrounds them like a self-imposed cloak.

Light as Life

In mankind, the true, the good, the beautiful are not only reflected but come to life. And again the scriptures teach of the inseparable connection—in fact, the eventual union in their highest forms—of light and life. "In [Christ] was life; and the life was the light of men" (John 1:4). And it is His light that "giveth life to all things" (D&C 88:13). And in man the inclusive *all* refers to the life of the mind and all the creative and responsive forces that are interwoven in him. A modern revelation speaks not only of the classic symbol "eternal life" but also of "eternal lives" (D&C 132:22–25), the plural emphasizing expansion and intensification of the lives within the whole person.

As the flourishing of plant life depends upon the light-nourishment traceable to the sun in the process of photosynthesis, so the light of the sun depends upon the Son of God. "He is in the sun, and the light of the sun, and the power thereof by which it was made" (D&C 88:7). In fact, one man records that the Prophet once said, "There is no light, except the Father and the Son" (Alfred Douglas Young diary, p. 5, in Church Historical Department). The nourishing that leads to the flowering of the soul—the crucial need of the soul—is His, and through Him ours. "I am come that they might have life, and that they might have it more abundantly" (John 10:10). Without Him we could not "abound," which is to say live, draw breath, survive. But to abound is to abide in Him, and to abide in Him, as vine to root, is to live abundantly.

When we are instrumental in transmitting this life-renewing power, we can be so drained that, like the Master or his modern prophets, our very "virtue" goes out and we are left visibly pale. "I became weak," said the Prophet after blessing nineteen children, "from which I have not yet recovered" (*Teachings*, p. 281). But when we are recipients of this power, it is the very "renewing of [our] bodies" (D&C 84:33), the reversal of all forms of distress, disease, disability, and degeneration, and the rekindling of our emotional life. In such times the effect in us is not only the opposite of darkness; it is the opposite of heaviness or burdensomeness. It is the essence of spiritual and physical buoyancy. "My burden is light" (Matthew 11:30).

In contrast, the soul-shrinking that occurs in the absence or withdrawal of light inevitably has to do with the heart's definition of life: love, and with love, joy and peace. It was John who recognized, as have few in history, that to hate is to be in darkness, and that conversely to love is to walk in the light (see 1 John 2:10–11). "Your minds in times past have been darkened," says a modern revelation, "because of . . . vanity and unbelief" (D&C 84:54–55). And vanity and unbelief are both ways of cutting ourselves from love, even from enlightened love of ourselves. The resulting condemnation is diminution of light, which blinds and numbs our capacities for the calm excitement of inspired love, the relish of joy, and the serenity of inner peace. We become, as Nephi told his brothers, "past feeling" (1 Nephi 17:45), and "the love of the Father shall not continue with [us]" (D&C 95:12). This, as the scripture earlier says, is the equivalent of "walking in darkness at noonday" (D&C 95:6), or, more technically, walking in noonday light, but afflicted with a darkness "that comprehendeth it not" (D&C 6:21). We literally die a little.

Even Temples

We began by saying that the universe is a combination of matter and of light or spirit, and that man himself is a microscopic universe. The Lord applies to us a more majestic word: *temples* (D&C 93:35). By divine design the temple is a microscopic man and man is a temple all alive. Standing on Mt. Scopus, northeast of Jerusalem, I was swept into a montage of images of temples— temples of Solomon, of Herod, of modern Kirtland and Nauvoo. I saw them built by the song of worthy sacrifice, endowed with encircling light and fire, and then violently desecrated, their veils ripped and trampled. Just so man, the living temple of God, can be a harmony of radiance or a divided shambles of darkness. In his vision of the future inhabitants of the holy city, John wrote:

And I saw no temple therein; for the Lord God Almighty and the Lamb are the temple of it.

And the city had no need of the sun, neither of the moon, to shine in it; for the glory of God did lighten it, and the Lamb is the light thereof. . . .

For the Lord God giveth them light; and they shall reign forever and ever. (Revelation 21:22–23; 22:5.)

To be light-magnified and light-purified is to have a foretaste of that temple of celestial personality: to begin to see as we are now seen by Him, and to know as we are now known by Him. And to enter that temple is to see God, the God of lights, born in us, the lightened god that is us. And as the temple is the fusion of all of heaven and earth, so within us the real, the true, the good, and the beautiful are to be blended in the prism of perfected personality. In Christ and through Christ, the singular sheen of saintliness will be swallowed up in the "eternal burnings" of godliness.

4

THE INTIMATE
TOUCH OF PRAYER

A ll of us need deeper understanding in prayer. All of us reach. All of us speak. But none of us have perfected the process and all of us need encouragement. Here is a portrait of the prayer life of the Prophet Joseph Smith. I'm convinced that as we feel our way into his life we will receive glimpses that are more vivid and helpful than if we simply read statements about what we ought to do—the Prophet's life gives us clear insight into what we *can* do.

There is a letter in the Prophet's handwriting written in 1832—only a few months after one of the most remarkable revelations he received. The record of that revelation is now section 46 of the Doctrine and Covenants. Joseph is writing to his wife, Emma.

> My situation is a very unpleasant one, although I will endeavor to be contented, the Lord assisting me. I have visited a grove which is just back of the town, almost every day, where I can be secluded from the eyes of any mortal, and there give vent to all the feelings of my heart in meditation and prayers. I have called to mind all the past moments of my life, and am left to mourn and shed tears of sorrow for my folly in suffering the adversary of my soul to have so much power over me, as he has had in times past. But God is merciful and has forgiven my sins, and I rejoice that he sendeth forth His Comforter unto as many as believe and humble themselves before Him." (Dean C. Jessee, ed., *The Personal Writings of Joseph Smith*

[Salt Lake City: Deseret Book Co., 1984], p. 238. Spelling and punctuation standardized.)

Now, that one paragraph is enough to tell us that he was struggling—blessed and magnified though he was—just as we are struggling with the weight of life, with the difficulties and weaknesses that are in us, and with the constant desire to receive of the Lord.

Some have asked in my hearing, "How is it that the Prophet Joseph Smith, age fourteen, could go into a grove, never before having prayed vocally (according to his own account, implying that he had prayed before in his heart), and that in that first prayer he received great and marvelous blessings—transcendent blessings? Does that mean that he simply had far greater faith than any of the rest of us?

One possible response to that is that the answer the Prophet Joseph Smith received wasn't just to his own prayer. I submit that it was to the prayers of literally millions, maybe those even beyond the veil who had been seeking and reaching for generations for the restoration of the gospel and the reestablishment of the kingdom of God on the earth. That suggests that you and I do not pray alone. We pray as part of a great modern movement, and we are united in that very process. I sometimes think that therefore we have some advantages that are not shared by others who have not yet found the gospel, found the authorities and gifts and blessings of the Holy Ghost, and found the crowning blessing of the priesthood.

Let me ask some elementary questions about Joseph Smith's prayer life to help us feel even closer to him, as his experience overlaps our own. Did the Prophet pray long or short? Was he, as we judge prayers, inclined to multiply words or was he inclined to be brief? The answer to that question is yes. There were times when the Prophet prayed briefly; there also were times when he stayed on his knees in prayer for a long time. Of the first, an example is an experience at Kirtland. The table has been set, and there is little to eat. He stands at the table and says, "Lord, we thank thee for this johnnycake and ask thee to send us something better. Amen." Shortly, someone knocks on the door, and there stands a man with a ham and some flour. The Prophet jumps to his feet and says to Emma, "I knew the Lord would answer my prayer." Well, that's a telegram prayer—that's very brief. (See Truman G. Madsen, *Joseph Smith the Prophet* [Salt Lake City: Bookcraft, 1989], p. 32.)

On the other hand Mary Elizabeth Rollins Lightner, a convert to the Church, only fourteen years of age at the time of the experience, describes coming with her mother to the Prophet's home, sharing in a small meeting where he set up a box or two and put a board across them to make room for people to sit. Now he spoke with great power. One of her comments is that his face, to her at least, "turned so white he seemed perfectly transparent." A great outpouring of the Spirit. But then he asked them to kneel. And he prayed. Such a prayer, she says, "I never heard before or since." So much did this prolong the meeting that some on the hard floor stood up, rubbed their knees a bit, and then knelt down again. It was long. (See Hyrum L. Andrus and Helen Mae Andrus, comp., *They Knew the Prophet* [Salt Lake City: Bookcraft, 1974], pp. 23–24.)

Did the Prophet address the Lord as *Father*, or did he have a special manner of address? Most frequently, the Prophet prayed "Our Father" or simply, "Father," or "O Lord," and was not inclined, as are some in our midst, to add adjectives and flowery phrases to that. I'm not saying that making such additions is wrong, but I note that he was intimate in prayer and that a simple "Father" was sufficient.

In counseling some missionaries he once said, "Make short prayers and short sermons." And he said on another occasion, "Be plain and simple, and ask for what you want, just like you would go to a neighbor and say, 'I want to borrow your horse to go to the mill.'" (*They Knew the Prophet*, p. 100.) That's plain. That's simple. And that's honest. So were his prayers.

There were times in sacred circumstances when the Prophet prayed in a formal way. I have in mind especially the unique situation of dedicating temples. Some people were upset and even left the Church through the experiences of the temple, either because so little occurred in their own experience or because so *much* did. The Prophet read the dedicatory prayer for the Kirtland Temple and announced that it had been given him by revelation. We have it recorded in Section 109 of the Doctrine and Covenants. That prayer has become the model, the archetype, if you will, for all subsequent temple dedication prayers. Some members were disturbed at that. First of all, they'd been taught that we don't have set prayers in our midst. The truth is that we have some. The Lord has not permitted us to modify the sacramental prayers—not by one word. They are set. And so also with the baptismal prayer.

Second, they were troubled that here was a man who had apparently been given these words to say by the Lord to whom he was to say them. That struck them as circular. But the Prophet elsewhere has taught us that, as President J. Reuben Clark put it, one of the things we should most often pray for is to know what we should most often pray for. At least half of the prayer process is our bringing our souls into receptivity so that we know what we ought to pray; we listen. There are direct statements in modern revelation, for example, about being given all things.

> He that is ordained of God and sent forth, the same is appointed to be the greatest, notwithstanding he is the least and the servant of all.
>
> Wherefore, he is possessor of all things; for all things are subject unto him, both in heaven and on the earth, the life and the light, the Spirit and the power. . . .
>
> But no man is possessor of all things except he be purified and cleansed from all sin.
>
> And if ye are purified and cleansed from all sin, ye shall ask whatsoever you will in the name of Jesus and it shall be done.

Then: "But know this, it shall be given you what ye shall ask." (D&C 50:26–30.) A sensitive, developing spiritual-minded person becomes more and more attentive and responsive to the Spirit and is able, therefore, to pray as the Prophet did. The Lord also said: "He that asketh in the Spirit asketh according to the will of God; wherefore it is done even as he asketh" (D&C 46:30). Thus we ought to follow the Prophet's lead, to listen and to pray with the Spirit; then the Spirit will prompt us both as to how we should pray and what we should say as we pray.

I've asked myself, "Did the Prophet sometimes pray for things never given or for guidance not allowed, or for privileges denied him?" He did. Like us, he sometimes struggled, and the Lord simply left that problem without solving it.

Two examples. The Prophet earnestly desired to know the time of the Savior's second coming. We've been taught no man knows the day nor the hour; but still, get a group of Mormons together, and after they admit that premise they say, "But, what do you think?" Well, the Prophet also wondered. He prayed very fervently to know, and the Lord's answer wasn't really an answer, except, "I won't tell you." It was: "Joseph, my son, if thou livest until thou art eighty-five years old, thou shalt see the face of the Son of Man; therefore let this suffice, and trouble me no more on this matter" (D&C 130:15). Joseph first assumed that that meant Christ would come in fifty-six years, which would have been when he, Joseph, would become eighty-five. But he realized that wasn't what he'd been told. He'd been told that if *he* lived to be eighty-five *he* would see the face of the Lord, and that might mean after dying. So he put down the only conclusion he could come to. "I believe the coming of the Son of Man will not be any sooner than that time" (see D&C 130:14–17; see also Diary of Oliver B. Huntington, p. 129, in Church Historical Department).

God simply doesn't want us to know the timing of the Second Coming. He wants us to go on living, I suggest to you, as if it were going to happen tomorrow. Spiritually speaking, that's what He wants from us—to be prepared. As He says, "I come quickly" (Revelation 22:20). But He also wants us to live our lives in a long-range way with inspiration and not in an unauthentic way, which some of our young people seem to follow. They say, "It's all going to blow up in our faces in five years, so why should I plan to go away to school?" That's not in keeping with the Lord's will.

On one occasion the Prophet was praying to know why our people had to suffer so in Missouri. A sorrowful letter he wrote them says, "He will not show [it] unto me" (*Teachings*, p. 34). There was at least one time earlier when he begged the Lord for what the Lord had told him He wouldn't give him. As we all do, the Prophet fell into the practice sometimes of saying, "Are you sure, Lord? Really, do you understand, Lord?" "I heard you, and the answer seems to be no, but are you sure?"

We remember the instance of Martin Harris. Twice the Prophet prayed asking for permission to lend Martin the manuscript. Twice the Lord said no. When the Prophet asked the third time, we might suppose he said or thought things like "But Lord, don't you understand, his wife is pushing him, Lord. What harm can it do? She needs to see something. She needs to have some reassurance." Well, there's a passage that says, "Seek not to counsel your God" (D&C 22:4).

Mother Smith recalled how Martin came to the house, paced up and down in front, hesitant to open the door to tell the truth. The Prophet saw him out the window. Finally he entered the house. "Martin, have you lost . . . ?" (See *History of Joseph Smith by His Mother,* pp. 127–29.)

For two weeks, the Prophet could not be comforted. He felt he had betrayed the Lord. And no one can conceive the joy that entered his heart when the revelation came, "Behold, . . . repent of that which thou hast done . . . and thou . . . art again called to the work." (D&C 3:9–10.) He said thereafter, and I think this was a summary of his experience, "I made this my rule: When the Lord commands, do it" (History of the Church 2:170). Well, he learned that, but he learned the hard way.

Did the Prophet practice family prayer? The answer is yes. During one period of the Prophet's life Eliza R. Snow served as a kind of baby-sitter in his home, and she wrote a poem called "Narcissa to Narcissus." She described how she admired the Prophet in public—that she saw him for what he was. But when she was in his home and though, knowing his greatness, saw him, as she puts it, as humble and unassuming as a child, kneeling in family prayer, she could not withhold her heart, and she loved his soul. The phrase "Narcissa to Narcissus," I believe, suggests that to see him, as with the mythological lad who looked in the water and saw his own reflection, enabled her to see herself. She came to a deeper sense of prayer in beholding him.

A brother who had never met the Prophet or his family came and was about to knock on the door, but hesitated because he heard singing. Sister Emma was leading the family and the guests, who were always numerous, in a kind of preparatory worship service. And then the Prophet prayed. (See *They Knew the Prophet,* p. 147.) He prayed three times a day with his family. And though in our lives it's difficult to get together once and overlap everyone, I nevertheless recommend that principle. Morning, noon, and night they had a kind of family prayer—beautiful!

Joseph once said, citing the book of Daniel, "You must make yourselves acquainted with those men who like Daniel pray three times a day toward the House of the Lord" (*Teachings,* p. 161). What's the significance of facing the temple? Apparently it can help recall both the promises the Lord has made to us in the temple and the promises we have made to Him—covenants in the House of the Lord. When President Wilford Woodruff dedicated the Salt Lake Temple he offered a specific prayer that people who had there committed their lives to the Lord Jesus Christ and were now assailed with temptation or trouble but were unable to get to the temple to supplicate the Lord might face the temple as they prayed, and that the Lord would honor their prayers. (See N.B. Lundwall, comp., *Temples of the Most High* [Salt Lake City: Bookcraft, 1966], p. 127.)

The Prophet, even in his own household, was templeminded both at Kirtland and at Nauvoo. The temple has been designated by the Lord himself as "a house of prayer" (D&C 88:119).

Did the Prophet pray when he was in desperate circumstances? Someone has said, intending it to be critical, that for some of us religion is like a spare tire—we never really put it on until we are in trouble. The Lord did indicate in a modern scripture that many in the day of peace and comparative well-being "esteemed lightly my counsel; but, in the day of their trouble, of necessity they feel after me." But He adds, "I will remember mercy." (D&C 101:8, 9.)

Well, the Prophet was in circumstances that were hard and difficult. Brigham Young once said of him: "Joseph could not have been perfected . . . if he had received no persecution. If he had lived a thousand years, and led this people, and preached the Gospel without persecution, he would not have been perfected as well as he was at the age of thirty-nine years." (*Journal of Discourses* 2:7.)

In one dramatic situation he was hauled out of his bed by four men one night and dragged on the ground, beaten, stripped, tarred and feathered. They attempted to poison him—because he clenched his teeth they failed to get the poison into his mouth, but it subsequently fell onto the grass and killed it. It was aqua fortis. A quack doctor who had his tools had threatened that he would emasculate the Prophet. He didn't. Even as they were at him like fiends, the Prophet vocally prayed to the Lord for deliverance. He did pray in extremity. My personal conviction is that the last words he spoke in this life were not, as some have supposed, a distress signal, but were a prayer: "O Lord, my God." These words, a few minutes later, Willard Richards repeated with hands uplifted as he thought of the condition of the Church in the loss of the Prophet.

Yes, Joseph prayed in extremity but he also prayed in great gratitude. And here is another insight. He taught the Saints that they should practice virtue and holiness, but that they should give thanks unto God in the Spirit for whatsoever blessing they were blessed with. In my own life, years have gone by, I'm sure, when I have offered prayers yet never spent an entire prayer simply to thank the Lord. My prayers have always had an element of asking, asking, asking. But Joseph taught the Saints that if they would learn to be thankful in all things—simply be thankful—they would be made glorious, and their prayers would take on a deeper, richer spirit.

The sin of ingratitude is one of the things that prevent us from as rich a prayer life as he had. He seemed to have an innate and deep capacity for gratitude, even for the slightest favor, from the Lord as from his fellowmen. And I have wept at times while reading that in his journal he sometimes wrote a kind of prayer for a brother. "Bless Brother So-and-So, Father, who gave me $1.35 today to help with such-and-such a project." Even the smallest favor called forth his warmth and gratitude.

Was the Prophet effective in silent prayers, did he commend that or even command it? I note with interest eight different places where the Lord, through the Prophet, says, "pray always." That's a strong imperative. How can we? If "pray always" means vocally, then none of us do it—none of us can. But if "pray always" includes the kind of prayer that is from the heart and wordless, we're getting closer to a possibility. And if it means, even more profoundly, that we are to be in the spirit of prayer regardless of what we may be doing, then all of us can pray always.

The Prophet gave us a better rendering of a New Testament verse about prayer. It is Romans 8:26. The King James Version of the Bible has Paul saying (speaking of how the Spirit can assist us in prayer), "The Spirit itself maketh intercession for us with *groanings* which cannot be uttered." The Prophet's version is, "The Spirit maketh intercession for us with *striving* which cannot be expressed (*Teachings,* p. 278). I think he is saying that when we have enough confidence in the discerning power of the Spirit, we stop worrying so much about the words we use and are concerned more simply to open up what is really deep in us—even things that we cannot find words for. Strivings are different than groanings—you can groan in discouragement and despondency and it can all be turned down instead of turned up, but strivings are upreaching. We can take our strivings—even those that we cannot express—and know that as we silently think and pour out our feelings, the Spirit will translate those and perfectly transmit them to the Lord. And in turn, the Spirit can respond from the Lord to us. A great confidence and a great freedom can come when we trust the Spirit for that.

The Prophet, as we know, became a learned man. He didn't begin so, but I occasionally wince a little when I hear people say, "Well, he was just an unlearned boy." How does one become learned? We say "go to school." What's a school? It's a place where there are teachers. Well, who were the Prophet's teachers? Not just the local schoolmarm or two in Palmyra. The Prophet Joseph Smith was taught face to face by some "minor" pedagogues like Moroni, Peter, James, and John, the ancient Apostles and prophets; and, if that weren't enough, the Father and the Son. It is not true to say that he was unlearned. He had the learning and wisdom of heaven. Who knows more about the epistles of Paul—professors who teach in graduate schools, or Paul?

We help ourselves in prayer by speaking aloud. It helps our minds stay on track. But there are advantages also to silent prayers and some kinds of mind wandering—letting the mind go in the direction that it seems to be impressed to go.

Now, just a word about the remarkable pattern the Prophet taught in the presence of priesthood brethren. This was a special kind of prayer circumstance in the Kirtland Temple. Here are his exact words: "I labored with each of these quorums [High Priests, Seventies, Elders] for some time to bring them to the order which God had shown to me, which is as follows: "The first part to be spent in solemn prayer before God, without any talking or confusion." (I take that to mean solemn, silent prayer.) "And the conclusion with a sealing prayer by President Rigdon" (that is, one man would then pray vocally with and for the group), "when all the quorums were to shout with one accord a solemn hosanna to God and the Lamb with an Amen, Amen, and Amen."

Notice, in passing, that we're warned by the Lord against vain repetition, but we are not warned against repetition. There are things we not only can but should repeat in our lives. And it is not correct to suppose that after you say something once, you mustn't ever say it again. Vain repetition is the kind of vanity of repeating without genuine concern, just supposing that saying a thing over and over from the neck up without any feeling is acceptable. No. But the Hosanna Shout, itself, is a repetition—three times we say hosanna, hosanna, hosanna. And three times we say amen. To continue: "Then all take seats and lift up their hearts in silent prayer to God, and if any obtain a prophecy or vision, to rise and speak that all may be edified and rejoice together."

Now, that is a special set of instructions, but the spirit of it, it seems to me, applies even to our own private prayers. Note that there is first a concentration, not confused but silent, then a vocal prayer, then a giving of gratitude, and then waiting upon the Lord with our hearts sensitive, and speaking, or at least, in private life, knowing what comes by the Spirit. Did that happen, that aftermath? Yes. The Prophet says in his journal: "The quorum of the Seventy enjoyed a great flow of the Holy Spirit. Many arose and spoke, testifying that they were filled with the Holy Ghost, which was like fire in their bones, so that they could not hold their peace, but were constrained to cry hosanna to God and the Lamb, and glory in the highest." (*History of the Church* 2:391–92.)

Of a similar occasion a few days before this one, Joseph said: "After these quorums were dismissed, I retired to my home, filled with the Spirit, and my soul cried hosanna to God and the Lamb, through the silent watches of the night; and while my eyes were closed in sleep, the visions of the Lord were sweet unto me, and His glory was round about me" (*History of the Church* 2:387). Much can be learned from that.

Half a century later, when forty years had passed since construction had begun on the Salt Lake Temple, the pattern the Prophet taught was used as Elder Lorenzo Snow led the Saints—some forty thousand of them—in the glorious privilege of uniting their voices in praise of the Lord that they had been able to reach the capstone. Forty thousand, and the shout was a *shout!* It echoed through the mountains. Can you imagine forty years of struggle and patience bursting out in joy as they did so! Well, that's acceptable to the Lord.

Another kind of shouting the Prophet rebuked. Let me in passing mention it. One time, Father Johnson asked a convert who had been a Methodist exhorter to pray in the family's evening worship. He hadn't overcome his habits. The exhorters in that old-time pattern were men who learned to throw their voice in a kind of falsetto quality. When the wind was right, they could be heard a mile away, some claim. This man began, literally, hallooing that way in prayer, and "alarmed the whole village." The Prophet was one of those who came running to the scene. In essence, he said, "Brother, don't pray like that again. You don't have to bray like a jackass to be heard of the Lord." (See *Journal of Discourses* 2:214.) Well, George A. Smith indicates that that brother left the Church. Now, if you're sincere, there's no problem. But there's something false and inconsistent about supposing that the Lord cannot hear you unless you halloo. He can hear the quietest turning of your own sacred conscience and knows the thoughts and intents of your heart.

The Prophet taught repeatedly that the Saints should be one in prayer, that when a group comes together in fasting and prayer, united in the petition of their hearts, that makes a greater difference somehow than if anyone alone had done so. The revelations say, "Be agreed as touching all things whatsoever ye ask of me" (D&C 27:18). Be one in your prayers, for "if ye are not one ye are not mine" (D&C 38:27). One of the sisters, the wife of George A. Smith, recalled the Prophet's statement to her. "He said that we did not know how to pray to have our prayers answered." But she added that when she and her husband received their endowments in the temple, they understood what he meant. (See *They Knew the Prophet,* p. 123.) The Lord instructed the Prophet to teach several of the brethren the keys whereby they might ask in prayer and receive an answer (see D&C 124:95, 97). Well, there is much about the privilege of the sanctuary that we cannot say outside the temple, but may I simply report that Brigham Young, who learned to pray listening to the Prophet, said repeatedly to the Saints that when someone prays in a congregation we should be saying in our minds what he or she is saying with the lips. We should repeat the very words in our minds, and then when we say amen we know what we're saying amen to. Without that repetition, sometimes we do not. Why is it important? So that the Saints may be one. Truly the effectual, fervent power of united prayer cannot be overestimated.

Later comment has to do with the original problem—the problem of guilt, the problem of sin. Here is the Prophet himself writing to his wife, saying, "I have called to mind all the past moments of my life and am left to mourn and shed tears of sorrow for my folly."

If we study them closely we find that all the Saints have had their struggles. Nephi, just to name one, writes with such strength in those first and early chapters that you wonder if he ever doubted or murmured or had a setback. The contrast between his attitude and even that of his own parents is startling. But in the fourth chapter of 2 Nephi, you will notice, he opens his soul and levels with us. And even though he has been struggling with the burden of leadership, he says, "When I desire to rejoice, my heart groaneth because of my sins." Then he prays with a power that reminds one of David in the Psalms, "O Lord, wilt thou encircle me around in the robe of thy righteousness . . . make a way for mine escape."

A homely illustration of the same point is the story about the two farmers talking, and there's a horse pulling the plow, but on his right flank every time he pulls, the strap rubs what has become an open gaping sore. The observer says, "Pretty tough on that horse to make him pull when he's got a gaping sore." The other farmer replies, "Yes, plumb tough, but I reckon we wouldn't get much work done in this world if we waited until everyone was plumb fit." And that's true in the Church. We wouldn't get any work done in the Church if we waited until all of us were perfect. The Lord wouldn't be able to call anyone to any position in the Church if he waited until we were all fully worthy.

If I may be personal for a moment, when I was called to be a mission president, the call was made by President Henry D. Moyle. I was taken aback by it, and surprised that he didn't ask any hard questions. I reminded him of that. "You haven't asked any questions of worthiness." He said, "Well, when one responds as you have, we don't have many questions." That didn't satisfy me. I said, "But President Moyle, I love the Church, but I have some problems." He came around the desk, put his arm around me, and said, "Brother Madsen, the Lord has to show a lot of mercy to let *any* of us work in His Church." That's true. But what does one do when he feels, as Lorenzo Snow put it, "that the heavens are as brass over his head" (see *Juvenile Instructor* 22:22). That though he ought to pray, he doesn't feel like praying. And when he does feel like praying, he is so ashamed that he hardly can. What then? My response is this glimpse from the Prophet.

The period just prior to the dedication of the Kirtland Temple saw an outpouring of the Spirit. Many of the brethren saw glorious visions, and the Prophet himself had a manifestation in which he saw, in panoramic vision, the lives of the Brethren of the Twelve—saw them in their strugglings, their flounderings, saw them preaching the gospel, saw them eventually brought back into the celestial kingdom. Interestingly, he saw them together—a group of them at least—as he recorded it, "in foreign lands." He didn't say England, but that's where they eventually went. He saw them, standing in a circle, beaten, tattered, their feet swollen, and clearly discouraged. Now, there are different levels of discouragement; we can be disturbed a bit, we can be worried, we can then be despondent, and there are moments in life for some of us when we ask, "What is the use?" And when we sink that far, we're almost to the point of wishing we could cease to be.

Well, the Prophet didn't indicate that it had gone that far with the Twelve, but they were looking down in their discouragement. Yet standing above them in the air was the Lord Jesus Christ. And it was made known to the Prophet that He yearned to show himself to them—to reach down and lift them—but they did not see Him. And the Savior looked upon them and wept. (See *History of the Church* 2:381.) We're told by three of the Brethren who heard the Prophet rehearse that vision that he could never speak of it without himself weeping. Why? Why would he be so touched? Because he knew that Christ willingly came into the world and took upon himself the pains and sicknesses of His people so that He might be filled with compassion so that all the Father's family could come to Him, if to no one else—and sometimes there is no one else—could come to Him, knowing that He knows what is taking place in us when we sin, or suffer affliction, or are discouraged. The great tragedy of life is that, loving us and having paid that awful price of suffering, in the moment when He is now prepared to reach down and help us we won't let Him. We look down instead of up, accepting the adversary's promptings that we must not pray; we cannot pray; we are not worthy to pray. But, says Nephi in response to that, "I say to you that ye must pray always, and not faint." (2 Nephi 32:8–9.)

There may be things that we are unworthy to do at times in our life, but there is one thing we are *never* unworthy to do, and that is pray. I have a testimony about this. The Prophet Joseph Smith not only taught it, but exemplified it. You *go* to the Lord regardless of the condition of your soul, and He will respond. He *never* closes the door against you. You may close it against Him, but if so that is your initiative, not His. We should call upon Him when we need Him most, and that's often when we feel least worthy, and then He can respond.

In the modern prophet Joseph Smith we have an example of living, breathing prayer—the kind that changes life. His early successes with prayer were the foundation of a pattern that brought him progressively closer to God. If prayer had no other function than to help us concentrate on the deepest concerns of our life—even to reveal ourselves to ourselves—it would be worth doing. But beyond that the Prophet illustrates for all time that prayer isn't just subjective, it isn't just self-hypnosis. Rather, it is a plan and pattern whereby we do in fact break through the veil and receive at the living hand of the living God through His Christ.

5

FORGIVENESS

The experience I relate first is well known in the Church. I want to share a few extra glimpses.

The one who had the experience was in the Quorum of the Twelve. As a junior member of that quorum he sat in a meeting in which the President of the Church (then John Taylor) asked his brethren for their vote to readmit into the Church a man who earlier had disgraced the Church. It is a complicated story. The man had not only committed a grievous sin but also, when confronted with it in the presence of the Twelve, had vehemently denied it. When finally he buckled and acknowledged his sin, he was excommunicated.

Considerable time had passed since then, and President Taylor now felt this man should have the privilege of beginning over. He asked his brethren. At first there was some feeling of "Oh no, is he really ready?" But over time, eventually, all the Quorum members except Heber J. Grant said yes. He alone said no.

In one of the later meetings at which this issue was discussed, President Taylor said to Elder Grant, "Why, Heber, why?" In substance, their exchange was as follows:

Elder Grant replied, "Because he stood up and lied!" That seemed to him almost more vicious than the sin.

Then President Taylor said: "But Heber, how will you feel when you stand before the Lord Jesus Christ hereafter, and it is clear that you were responsible for keeping this man outside the Church?"

That didn't slow Elder Grant down at all. He said: "Why, I will look Him in the eye and say: I *am* responsible for keeping that man out of the Church!"

President Taylor smiled and said: "Well, Heber, stay with your convictions! Stay right with them!"

When Elder Grant went home that day, while waiting for lunch he opened the Doctrine and Covenants, as it happened turning to section 64. He read: "I, the Lord, will forgive whom I will forgive, but of you it is required to forgive all men" (D&C 64:10).

That's tough enough. *All* is an inclusive word, isn't it? There is no exception. But the revelation also says, "he that forgiveth not his brother his trespasses standeth condemned before the Lord; for there remaineth in him the greater sin" (D&C 64:9).

My first question on this is "Greater than what?" Are we to say, for example, that a woman who refuses to forgive her husband of adultery has committed a more serious sin than adultery? The sin of this man, who lied about it, was that, a moral sin; and yet, taken at its face value, the above verse seems to say, "It's worse not to forgive."

Well, one of the great things about Elder Grant was that when he knew he was wrong, he was wrong; and he was a practitioner of what Brigham Young called instant repentance. He brought his hand down hard on the book—so characteristic of him—and said aloud so his wife could hear: "Well, that settles it. If the devil himself repents, I'll baptize him!"

Now the sequence. He went right back down to the Church Office Building. He had to see President Taylor. He explained to him that he had changed his mind and wanted this man baptized into the Church. President Taylor was pleased. He laughed his Lancashire British Santa Claus laugh and then asked, "Heber, what happened?"

Elder Grant told him. He had opened the Doctrine and Covenants accidently to that passage. Now we are getting to the psychological.

"Heber, how did you feel this morning at the meeting?" (where he alone stood up in opposition). "How did you feel about this brother?"

He said: "I felt like I wanted to go out and knock him down!"

"That's right, you did. Now Heber, how do you feel now?"

Elder Grant started to weep. "To tell the truth" (and I think it was a little bit of a surprise to him) "To tell the truth, President Taylor, I hope the Lord will forgive the man."

President Taylor said: "Heber, I put it to the vote so that you"—and I think he mentioned one or two others—"might learn what you have here learned today. This morning you did not have the Spirit of the Lord Jesus Christ. This afternoon you do. Never forget that, Heber!"

Elder Grant learned to forgive essentially because it was a commandment. It is in the scriptures. He had always sustained the scriptures. They said we should forgive everyone. He did it. That's not quite the same as learning to forgive *because you profoundly need forgiveness yourself.*

The problem with being as good a man and as righteous a man as Heber J. Grant is that one tends to lack compassion for those who have all kinds of problems with doing what to oneself is easy. But he later learned that; he had condemned one of his own brethren, accused him, and in effect said, "You are not doing what you ought to do in this matter." Then he came to realize that it was he and not the other man who wasn't doing what he should. And then he went in abject humility, threw his arms around the man, and pleaded for his forgiveness, and asked for his encouragement and help in repenting. Heber J. Grant was a more compassionate man after that.

It is implicit in Elder Grant's final reaction that even though he complied out of a sense of "I will obey because I am commanded," in the moment he did it, it sank into him; it changed him.

I recall the essence of a statement made years ago by Elder Jeffrey Holland in a Young Special Interest Multi-Regional Conference. He started by saying that forgiving others is the hardest thing required of us by the gospel of Jesus Christ. But we ought not to feel particularly sorry for ourselves that it is hard. He went on to say in a way I cannot duplicate that when some Roman had driven the spikes at the Crucifixion, of all the things Jesus the Christ might have thought or said, either in prayer or in outreach through others, the least likely from a mortal point of view is that the expression of His thought and heart would be to plead for forgiveness for the crucifiers. That is Christlike in the ultimate sense! The miracle is that we have the power—we, mere men and women—to do that. But this doing isn't exactly an act—it's an inward doing that changes everything.

Now, may I digress for a minute with a few implications and then come back to our whole concern, which is, How can we do more to help our loved ones and ourselves become forgiving, as well as forgiven, in the recognition that somehow these two are inseparably linked?

First, a philosophical implication. People used to come to Joseph Smith and ask questions, and I would that someone had been around with a tape recorder. In the Nauvoo period some came and asked him a hard question. The controversy was between egoism and altruism. In its ultimate form egoism maintains that what we all are doing, when you get down to the basics, is seeking our own satisfaction! This view, psychological egoism, holds that no one ever acted in the interest of others. If he seemed to, that was all on the surface; at root, all motives are self-serving.

The opposite view is altruism, which means that at least *some* of our acts—and there are those who maintain it is possible that *all* of them—are not in the end self-serving but are other-serving, so that even those things that appear to be the mere gratification of self—eating, drinking, sleeping, whatever—and all the separate complications of those, turn out in the end to be an effort to help others.

Now, what these brethren wanted to know from the Prophet was, Is it wrong to seek your own satisfaction? Is the principle of self-aggrandizement wrong? The classic answer, one of the most illuminating things I have ever read in Mormon literature, is the Prophet's reply, according to Oliver B. Huntington, who was there. It is this:

Joseph acknowledged "that some people entirely denounce the principle of self-aggrandizement as wrong," but "it is a correct principle," But it—that is our concern that we have accomplished something for our own ultimate glory—"may be indulged upon only one rule or plan—and that is to elevate, benefit and bless others first." That's one version. Another version, not quite that strong, is "seek to elevate and enoble others also." "If you will elevate others, the very work itself will exalt you. Upon no other plan can a man justly and permanently aggrandize himself." Those two adverbs suggest to me that it is possible temporarily and unjustly to aggrandize yourself; but permanently, no. (See *They Knew the Prophet,* p. 61.)

It seems to me that many of us suppose that all absolutes are obsolete! Under pressure, I would personally defend as an absolute law what I have just said. You can rephrase it as you wish, but it would come down to something like this: "It is impossible, worlds without end, to achieve your own fulfillment without the explicit and conscious inclusion of others. If you ignore, reject, or trample down others, in the long run you will absolutely and always fail." That's the gospel of Jesus Christ.

Now, a theological version of that. Does not the Lord's Prayer say that we are to pray: "Forgive us our debts, as we forgive our debtors"? (Matthew 6:12.) Have you ever wondered about that linkage? Why didn't he simply tell us to pray and ask to have our *own* debts forgiven? He asks us to pray in such terms that we could almost put it in this negative way: "Father, forgive us to that degree and only to that degree that we forgive others." That's a prayer which, if answered at all, would in some cases evoke a negative answer. The positive way is: "Father, because I have reached that point in my life where I have a broken heart and a contrite spirit, because I have seen my weaknesses and my need I yearn to forgive all others! Including my enemies"—and the point is reached where it isn't just "including; it is *especially* my enemies." Why? Because they are the ones that are bearing the heaviest burdens of unforgiveness.

Christ did set that pattern. He is our paradigm. It has always interested me that the reason the woman taken in adultery isn't stoned is that Jesus appeals to the conscience of those around Him: "Who among you is really justified?" That is what He is saying, and it interests me psychologically that He didn't stand up and put His chin up, saying: "Which one of you dares to throw a rock!" That's probably the way some of us might have done it. He wasn't even facing them. He was stooping down, writing in the sand. Some people think He was writing the Ten Commandments at the same time and then saying: "Which of you would say that you have. . . ." But their faces and their attitudes were not in His vision. They could slink away one by one and not have to question whether they were defying His defiance. I think the Master was a Master.

So only He was left with her. "Woman, where are thine accusers?" He said, so as to underline "I do not condemn thee, go thy way and sin no more." The actual sequence of events, I think, is not that she first made radical restitution, proving what we all like to talk about, the four or five or six R's of repentance, and then having paid the full price, she is confronted by Jesus, who says: "You're off the hook now. You paid." Not exactly that. It's as if He forgives her *first* as the *foundation* for her repentance. The Joseph Smith Translation says: "And the woman glorified God from that hour, and believed on his name." (JST John 8:11.) It seems that from the moment she tasted the power of divine forgiveness, she repented.

Now, the reason I don't want to dwell on that is that it may be out of phase, that may not be quite the way the Lord wants us to understand the sequence. So as far as His forgiveness is concerned, we are taught, He went through it *all* to earn the right and to have the power to forgive. So far as *our* forgiveness is concerned, He keeps saying we have to forgive everybody. Everybody.

How much do we have to forgive?

Everything.

For how long do we have to forgive?

Just all the time.

After we clean the slate and get up to today, what if people go on deliberately, maliciously repeating the transgressions against us?

Answer: Continue to forgive.

The Prophet Joseph Smith said once in a sermon: "We have not yet forgiven [some people] seventy times seven, as our Savior directed; perhaps we have not forgiven them once." (*Teachings*, p. 238.)

I turn to the really important issue and I have to bear testimony to the truth of our own need and of the impact this can have in seeking the health and wholeness of those around us. It is remarkable that we are told not to forgive is a serious transgression. It is remarkable further that, in a way, sons of perdition, sons of darkness, are those who have *deliberately* and *knowingly* rejected Christ. How much do they really know? The Prophet said the symbol of that is standing out in the noonday sun saying the sun is not shining. To put this even more concretely, he said a person cannot commit the unpardonable sin unless he knows absolutely what he is doing. "He has got to deny the Holy Ghost when the heavens have been opened unto him " (*Teachings*, p. 358.) Now, that indeed is a slamming of the door against God with a permanence and a depth of understanding that defies our present comprehension.

In Section 132 of the Doctrine and Covenants the question is raised, What is unpardonable? The answer: "Wherein ye shed innocent blood" (v. 27). Now we have the explanation of what that phrase means. Whose blood? Jesus Christ's! But how could one do that? He has lived and died in this mortal time. "You assent," says the verse. "You assent [you agree with, you consent] unto my death." Elsewhere in the scriptures that is called "crucifying the Son of God unto themselves" (see D&C 76:35). In this case it isn't just a matter of killing a body, which is all the Romans saw. It is, in effect, wanting to render null and void, so far as you are concerned, what He did as to body, spirit, and mind or intelligence. It is, in effect, to say: "I prefer to serve Master Mahan, and I refuse to accept what you have done." Now, notice that this is not an act but *is* a sin, a most horrifying sin of the mind. It is something one does inside. My suggestion for our thoughts and prayers is, Isn't radical unforgiveness of others of the same caliber of sin?

If one commits murder in an act of passion, that may take five minutes; but if twenty-four hours a day, waking and sleeping, you go on holding grudges, harboring hostile feelings, this is a kind of self-contradiction. You may have reached that point of desperation in your own life when you have prayed and yearned to have the monkey off your back—your guilt and your sin—and maybe you sense that a half-measure of forgiveness has come from the Lord. But then you turn and say: "But not him! Don't you forgive him! I'm not going to; he doesn't deserve it!" Thus you then close the channel of love and compassion and revelation from the Lord. It is like triple plate steel against water. It cannot get through to us.

Now, seriously, how soon can you say to yourself: "Your unforgiveness is worse than your husband's (or wife's) sin"; or, "Your attitudes towards your father built up over thirty years are really more soul-shrinking than anything he ever did or didn't do."

That's strong, but it's right! I submit that it's true! We alone are responsible for allowing into our hearts the poison of unforgiveness. We have power that moment, gloriously, to see that this person we have thought of as the cause of our sins is himself suffering. We take on that glorious attitude of the Master.

A simple illustration is the story told of Lord Byron. He's walking down the street, and here's a bully beating a smaller man until the welts rise, apparently just to be doing it. People are around, watching, some of them with alarm and some of them with a kind of strangely satisfying fascination. And the man goes on and on with it.

Byron comes to the man and says, "How long are you going to go on beating him?"

The bully turns and says, "What's that to you?"

He replies with tears in his eyes, "Because if you will let him go, I will take the rest of it."

The story of a woman I know illustrates all that I have been trying to convey. She hated her husband, but by counseling she was able to come to see what he was going through; this was not yet forgiveness, but the concern to somehow relieve him came to her like a wave. Jesus said we are to forgive our enemies, and we have been unaware that often our enemies are our loved ones. Categories get mixed, and the person we love the most we hate the most. But when we deeply forgive others we throw it all off and say, "No more will I nurse and brood that poison in any degree." The magnificent change in us is that then, sometimes for the first time, we believe and feel *we* have been forgiven.

We then belong to the family of the Lord Jesus Christ. In a sense we take on burdens similar to His. He didn't deserve it! He didn't have it coming! He had every right to say to mankind: "What right have you . . . ?" Similarly, in many cases we do not deserve what we get at the hands of others in this world of pain and affliction. But that is beside the point. The point is that whatever has happened, we must forgive; and the law is, when we do we will feel a blessed forgiveness of ourselves from the Lord himself.

Faith and testimony tell us it is worth everything to go on seeking, to cleanse and purify our lives, to repent. I submit that the core of that is the power to forgive; that the core of that is the power to receive forgiveness. And the proper word at the end of that is *grace*. As we progressively keep God's commandments we "shall receive grace for grace" (D&C 93:20). One meaning of that is that we will receive as much grace—free, unearned, unmerited blessedness from the Lord Jesus Christ—as we are willing to give to others. Grace for grace. May God help us to catch that vision, to recognize that love day by day cannot endure—I don't think it can last a day—unless there is forgiveness, reciprocal forgiveness.

There comes to my mind the punchline from the movie *Love Story,* which was not a real love story. Part of the line is "Loving is not having to say you are sorry." Perhaps that has an occasional application, but my own conviction is different. With all my soul I say it is precisely the opposite. When you really love, you instantly say "I'm sorry" when you have hurt the beloved.

I once thought the Atonement was over. Of course, in one important sense it is. It happened, it is locked in the New Testament era. Jesus did say on the cross "It is finished." But as I read the scriptures we cannot say that at that moment Jesus' suffering ceased forever. In one way His suffering has increased since the Garden of Gethsemane. That one way is obvious to any of us. After having paid that terrible price in an agony that is beyond our power to comprehend, He now must face the sorrow of God's children being heartless, cold, calculating, and indifferent. He sees us with His own compassion and knows how desperately we need mercy; yet He has to bear the burden of knowing that the reason mercy is not operative in our lives is that we ourselves lock it out. "All eternity is pained" (D&C 38:12). All eternity is embodied in Jesus Christ, and even now He suffers. But I know of no place in scripture where He announces that because of that He is giving up, or that because our sins have become so extreme He will refuse forgiveness to the penitent. He promises that forgiveness is always there, and this is a joyous thought. But along with the joys both here and hereafter there will always be a measure of sorrow.

Yes, in worlds ahead all of the righteous will experience a measure of pain and sorrow for the sins of the world. It will be part of our destiny, as with the three Nephites (see 3 Nephi 28:9). But that very sorrow can lead to mercy and forgiveness and redemptive love.

6

HUMAN ANGUISH
AND DIVINE LOVE

The subject of this chapter is not a question or problem, not an academic toy. It is the human predicament, as we can show with three illustrations:

1. An irreverent but it seems to me downright honest critic of Christianity argues, in effect: "If a child is born to me healthy and bright-eyed, you tell me, God loves you. If a child is born without a spine, or hopelessly paralyzed, you tell me, God still loves you. Frankly, that kind of love I can do without. If God causes or permits events that my worst mortal enemy would not permit, then the idea of both 'God' and 'love' are absurd."

2. One day my family sat watching the big screen production of *The Greatest Story Ever Told*. There you see a sinister Herod send his soldiers to Bethlehem. Then come the screams of mothers, glimpses of blood-smirched swords pulled from children's bodies. Then you see Mary and Joseph, who have received divine warning, walking peacefully with their Babe toward the safety of Egypt. As this scene closed, the hand of my little girl came into mine and she whispered, confused and frightened, "Daddy, didn't Heavenly Father care about those other children?"

3. Third is the universal outcry of our own souls in tribulation. "Why?" and "Why me?" We speak much of worthiness

and blessedness—and of keeping the laws that result in both. But there is, in this cry, the sense of what some call "frustrated entitlement." We have, in measure (not perfectly, but close enough), kept the law; and we aspire through dark and dawn to do better. We feel a certain inner worthiness, a sense of "deserving better." But no better comes. Only worse. And still worse. Others we think of as less worthy seem to prosper. We do not demand ease. But we sense injustice, and we crave, alas, a little mercy. And how long can we hold on to this slipping rope and pray in faith, let alone in love?

All this supposes that God both can and should prevent such misfortunes; that, indeed, a good and loving God would.

Let us look at the "can" before we look at the "should."

In a seminar at Harvard we were devoted to the analysis of St. Augustine's writings. And if you've read any of Augustine's confessions, you're aware that his early life, to say the least, was a traumatic and guilty one (much more so, incidentally, than Joseph Smith's). In his doctrine of creation, Augustine begins with a premise that God is all-powerful. To him that means that all things—all else beside God, including space, time, and the souls of men—were created by God from nothing. The puzzle arises as to why a being of unlimited power should have chosen to create such a universe as this: of pain, torment, and (on some views) endless damnation. Specifically, evil and the devil were among the realities God chose to create. Why, being good, could He—would He—do such a thing?

This eventually led Augustine to the topic of freedom. How was it that God could make us from nothing and yet condemn us or reward us for actions? Why hold us responsible when He alone is responsible? "For," said one student in the class, "a God who is totally the cause of what is, is indirectly the cause of everything one does." At this point I raised my hand and said with a measure of restraint, "Isn't it at least conceivable that man is not totally the creation of God?" There was a roar of disapproval, and students began to hammer at me from both sides. When things quieted down, the professor said, "Well, the idea cannot be ruled out arbitrarily." But the idea is ruled out by the major wings of Christianity. Otherwise, on their view God would not be absolute.

Actually, as soon as it is recognized, as in modern revelation it is, that there is more than one eternal will in the universe—indeed, an infinity of such wills or autonomous intelligences—we have cut the thread that supposes God can "do anything." In all-important ways even He, the greatest of all, can only do with us what we will permit Him to do. Our center selves can agree or disagree, assent or resent, cooperate or oppose. To say, as the scriptures do, that God has all power and that He is almighty and that with Him all things are possible is to say that He has all the power and might it is possible to have in this universe of multiple selves.

And as soon as it is recognized, as in modern revelation it is, that there are eternal inanimate things which are subject to laws, to "bounds and conditions" which God did not create but himself has mastered, we have cut another thread of illusory omnipotence. For on the extreme view of His power, whatever purpose He may have had in creating everything from nothing, those same results could have come if He had created nothing from everything. To say "that is impossible" is to say with the Mormon that God cannot "do just anything." He can do only what our wills and eternal laws will permit. In short, He did not make us from nothing, and what He makes of us depends on us and the ultimate nature of a co-eternal universe.

Thus we make it too simple when we say in an hour of stinging misfortune, "Couldn't God have prevented this?" The related issue is, ought He to? The "bounds and conditions" mean that if He prevents this He cannot achieve that.

For example, growth, expansion, development. We can only grow with stress and distress. There is no muscle without strain, no character without the fiery trials of action and conflict. "There must needs be opposition" not only implies an eternal resistance in the nature of things; it also implies that man needs opposition in order to become what he has it in him to become.

So much on the "can."

Now on the "should."

Our outcry supposes that if we really were in charge, these things would never happen. But is that completely the case? Did we come into the world "without our own permission"? On the contrary.

We chose knowingly to enter our present state or sphere of existence. That's a fascinating idea. You may have heard a teenager who says shiftily, "I did not ask to be born," to which it can be truly replied, "Oh, yes, you did." There's another answer you can indulge for comic relief. When your child says, "I didn't ask to be born," you can say, "If you had, the answer would have been no."

We did knowingly elect, and not only choose and elect but also prepare for this world with its real risks, its real opportunities, and its real promises. And those who say they are in their second childhood are unwittingly speaking the truth.

The question thrown upward, "Why did you get me into this?" needs translation: "Why did I get me into this?"

Imagine, for a moment, what it might be like to have a close, intimate friend who is sworn to stand by you and protect you, and maybe even die for you. Suppose he is a native of a foreign country and has never heard of modern surgery.

If he were ushered into a room where you were undergoing an appendectomy, saw the doctors and nurses cutting away and the evidences of blood and pain, he would likely jump to three conclusions:

1. That these persons were trying to torture you, perhaps take your life.
2. That all this was being done against your will.
3. That the highest service he could render you would be to pull them off.

But, you see, he would not only be mistaken; his assumptions would, in fact, be the exact opposite of the truth. These highly trained persons are intent on helping you. Truly, they could spare you the pain of the operation; but only at the cost of your life. It is at your request; and your willingness, even anxiety, to "go through with it," however you might shrink, led you to sign a statement justifying any medical action they deemed proper while you were still incapable of further instructions. (You might even have cautioned them: "Don't pay any attention to my groans. Do what you have to do.") And third, the worst thing he could do would be to prevent or even to interrupt their carrying out their task.

Life is an obstacle course. And sometimes it is a spook alley. But the before was a time of visioning the after. And some of our prayers are like the gamblers', "Give me the money I made you promise not to give me if I asked for it." What does a true friend do in such a case? God will honor our first request, to let us go through it; and He will provide us (let Him) with the way to make it bearable. More, to make it productive.

The Punitive Theory

Now, let me mention the theory about evil that we all theoretically reject. In practice it often still clings to us. We deny it of others, suspect it of ourselves. It's the so-called "punitive" theory of evil, to the effect that whenever someone suffers, it is because he deserves to. All misfortune is the product of sin. We "had it coming."

To be autobiographical for a moment, I recall an early clean-cut instance of temptation and submission. As a small fry, by jimmying my bank with a screwdriver I recovered my small fortune of seventeen cents, went to the store, and bought fig newtons. (You know, Augustine worries about the fact that he once stole pears. He spends a whole chapter on the question, what motivated him to steal? "Why did I do it?" My problem was figs.) While I was riding home on my tricycle—I must have been five or six—a hose or something in the sidewalk upset my bike; I tipped over and badly scuffed my knee. What was my first thought? Yes, you know very well. So with all of us. And I submit that though you are now mature and no longer believe that all mishaps and suffering are retribution, still the thought lingers. "What have I done to deserve this?" Sometimes that is an appropriate question, and there is an answer. But I want to talk about the instances where the answer is not that you have in fact deserved it, but something else.

Now, since I've mentioned a classical theory, let me mention three others, which, as I believe, are misleading, even or especially when they contain a kernel of genuine insight.

Is Evil "All in Your Mind"?

One theory which arises and is motivated by supreme reverence for the perfection of God is what is called the illusory theory; that all we call "evil" is but the phantom of our minds. It is not real. God, this view reasons, is perfect. Therefore, His creation is perfect. But there is nothing He did not create. Therefore, everything is perfect. This is the nerve of Christian Science, and is characteristic of certain kinds of absolute idealism and certain strains of Buddhism. All concrete suffering is addressed with: "It's all in your mind. You are a victim of error. If you saw aright, you would know that this world is perfect."

One reason why this will not hold up is that in a perfectly good universe even the illusion of evil would not be present. We are imperfect in seeing it otherwise. Admit that imperfection and then why not others? Some of us, in moments of puppy-love, may have heard impatient people say: "But you're not really in love. You just think you're in love." And we may have walked away saying to ourselves: "Maybe so. But to me it could not have more impact if it were real." Haven't you ever wanted to say in response to, "It is all in your mind," "I would rather have it almost anywhere else"? Some mental illness is more resistant to treatment than physical.

Now, there may be certain things we call evil that are not, and vice versa. But that theory is not adequate.

Is It "The Point of View"?

A second theory is the perspective theory, especially evident in Leibniz and satirized by the Voltaire of *Candide*, a book that is painfully funny. What does Leibniz say? He says, as Browning does at the end of his poem, "God's in his heaven, all's right with the world." Under the aspect of eternity, the view of God, the "evil" is acceptable because this is the "best of all possible worlds." Evil is "compossible" with good to achieve a greater good. To which Bertrand Russell replies, "How do we know that good is not in the world to achieve a greater evil?" This theory differs from the illusory theory because it implies that if you get out of perspective, evil is really there. There is common sense support for this. If the Venus de Milo was on a stand in your home, and you walked up to it and put your nose right against the base, you would see something, but it would hardly be beautiful. On the other hand, if you recede too far in the distance, you only see a gray cylinder on the horizon. Again, beauty is lost. But from the proper perspective the Venus de Milo is beautiful, even without her arms.

By the same token, a man with a magnifying glass can look at the nose of his girl. But he shouldn't, unless he wants to see a volcanic field. In aesthetics there is a famous theory by Bullough which talks about psychic distance. He uses a clever analogy. Suppose you suddenly see a fire on the dark horizon. You drive closer. The clouds hang over it in a majestic way, and the eerie colors of the flames play on people's faces and on the firemen with their hoses and ladders. This calls for a camera. It's magnificent. But if you happen to be the owner of the uninsured house, all of that beauty is lost on you. Perspective does make a difference.

One problem is: We don't have God's perspective. And Leibniz offers us few suggestions on how we can come closer to it.

The Privative Theory

Another view is the official theory of the Roman Catholic Church. It's called the privative theory. Essentially, it's an attempt to exonerate God from creating evil. It says that evil is not a positive reality, but is the absence of good. Now, that is a bit puzzling until you realize that the absence is not in vacuo, it is an absence in something. If, therefore, I call you evil, what I really mean on this theory is that you lack or are deprived of certain kinds of goodness. The devil is a privative being. He just isn't any good.

How satisfactory is that? Not very, I'm afraid, if what one wants is either comfort or conquest. For if anyone had said to me, as I lay in the hospital on one occasion, that I was not really experiencing pain but only the absence of pleasure, I would have wanted to throw him out as a mockingbird.

Evil does have positive effects, positive force in the world, like it or not. Hate begets hate, just as love begets love.

Privative evil (for example, ignorance) is only one kind of real evil.

The Instrumental Theory

This leads up to a view which, I think, is at the center of the restored gospel. It is sometimes technically called an instrumental theory. It does not say all pain is the result of transgression, nor deny its reality, nor resort to perspective or privation. Evil, suffering, and stress are seen as eternal. They will not be destroyed, but can be utilized. They can be instruments to something good. Indeed, the highest work of suffering is a work of perfection—godliness.

The Lord's Way

But let us bring this insight down to loam soil.

In the original of the letter Joseph Smith wrote from Liberty Jail (it belongs with Psalms—a masterpiece of religious writing) are several moving insights which precede the deeper one. For one thing, the Prophet is told that "thine adversity and thine afflictions shall be but a small moment" (D&C 121:7). That "small moment" turned out to be five more years of incredible struggle. But comparatively, it was a small moment. That, I submit, is a real force in facing suffering. To believe—better, to know—that this lonely or crushed or deprived or painwracked condition won't last forever, that it will somehow, somewhere be over, is a balm of comfort. Without it, certain kinds of suffering would indeed be unbearable.

Then the Lord says, "Thou art not yet as Job." Here we have the "It could be worse" appeal. Always it could be. Says a Persian legend, "I complained that I had no shoes until I saw a man who had no feet." A little bit of chiding comes through in the Lord's reminder and promise that, unlike the situation of Job, "Thy friends do stand by thee, and they shall hail thee again with warm hearts and friendly hands." (Vv. 9, 10.) Some friends are the wrong kind and add to our burden. They come in and say: "All right, Job. Let's have it! What have you done wrong?" "Job's comforters," they're called. No comfort. Job didn't have the memory of awful transgressions. The roof fell in on a loving, righteous man. That was redramatized in MacLeish's modern play *JB*. A literary critic said, "The thing that amazed me was to see JB, after it's all over, say, 'All right, let's start again,' not knowing but what the whole roof would fall in again." That is the tingle and threat of Job's life. And of ours. But those of us with faithful friends are always better off than he.

Nietzsche is often classified as an anti-Christ. But Nietzsche saw some things more clearly than his religious friends. For several years he had a continual toothache. He talked about "eternal recurrence." And his attitude was heroic. He arose each morning, set his jaw, and said, "Once more." He had the courage to go on. He would not be weak, would not yield to it, and was "grateful for small mercies." That is Jobian trust.

There is an "if" clause in the Lord's answer. "If" what? "If thou endure it well" (D&C 121:8). The original, I'm impressed to say, says "If thou art faithful and endure it well." Faithful. Faith-full. That makes a great difference. "If thou art called to pass through tribulation" (D&C 122:5).

I know many people who comfort themselves with what technically is "Deism"—the absentee landlord conception of the Lord; that He "wound up" the universe and then turned His back on us, and consequences fall without intervention.

If that outlook helps anyone, I would be the last to seek to overturn it. It does seem to me that the message of this letter qualifies it, for the Lord says, "their bounds are set, they cannot pass" (v. 9). Who were bound? Joseph's enemies, his betrayers, his "false brethren"—all men. They could only go so far. Some will say such a promise is not made to us. But it is.

Indeed, promises have been given (yes, many are conditional) that require the Lord to be very close. One day when I was on an airplane we hit some terribly rough air. The wings were swaying, it seemed, like seagulls. Even the flight attendants became alarmed, and that only distressed the passengers more. I was reading, feeling very calm. When I asked myself why, it was because of a promise given me in a blessing that, in effect, while in the path of duty I would travel safely, "whether on land, sea, or air." Musing about that, it seemed to me apparent that either the Lord had adequate foreknowledge that no airplane (which must include this airplane) would crash with me aboard. Or, lacking that foreknowledge, He yet had such power that in the event such a disaster were imminent He would somehow intervene and prevent it.

Take either or both of those alternatives and apply them to the thousands (millions?) of inspired promises made to the Lord's covenant people (even scriptural generalizations such as "If you will . . . then I will"). It means His power and knowledge in our lives are much more intimate and ever-present than we tend to dream. He may, indeed, be closest when we suppose Him to be farthest away.

The Glorification of Experience

The most vital and, in some ways, miraculous insight of all (and the most trying, perhaps, to our faith and love) is this: that after describing a whole catalog of anguish which, either previously, then, or later, the Prophet faced, including betrayal, and having his young son thrust from him by the sword, and having "all the elements combine to hedge up the way" (have you ever felt like that, when everything goes wrong?), and seeing the heavens "gather blackness," and having "the very jaws of hell gape open the mouth," the Lord reveals the pearl of great price:

> Know thou, my son, that all these things shall give thee experience, and shall be for thy good. The Son of Man hath descended below them all. Art thou greater than he? (D&C 122:7–8.)

What good, we may ask, could possibly be served by such affliction?

Brigham Young said of Joseph (and leaving out the fact that, as John Taylor wrote, he has done more, save Jesus only, for the salvation of man than any other man who ever lived) that he suffered more in thirty-eight years than many men could in one thousand; that loosing one thousand hounds on Temple Square after one jackrabbit "would not be a bad illustration of the situation of the times of the Prophet Joseph" (*Journal of Discourses* 10:315; see also 2:7); but that he was more perfected, more sanctified, more glorified because, in Joseph's words, "I have waded in tribulation lip-deep; but every wave of adversity which has struck me has only wafted me that much nearer to Deity."

The Prophet teaches and embodies this marvelously. Hence, it is not enough to endure stoically. Many religions and individuals have based themselves primarily on stoicism. Spinoza did. Under that discipline you endure only because you're saying to yourself, "It had to be." Why? "Stark necessity." That can keep you alive in a prison camp or in the loss of vital organs. It has been known to. "It has to be. Face it. It's necessary." That is resignation, a kind of fatalism. But it's not enough. The greater thing is to endure suffering with faith in the Son of Man, which enables it to yield its perfect result, which means the fulness of the powers of godliness.

Now, let me briefly address two immediate objections. It has been said that too easily this view of suffering slips into asceticism; that is, to the notion that the more one suffers, the better he is. Soon he is led to take the initiative: to deny himself, to sit on nails, to refuse himself normal appetites. Elements of asceticism can be found in both Catholic and Protestant traditions, and even more in Eastern religions. Hence the *New Yorker* magazine cartoons showing emaciated men reclining on stones or nails. Do we take the position that this is desirable? No. Mormonism is not ascetic. It does not recommend that you suffer by your own hand.

I want to mention one anecdote: A brother, who shall remain nameless, during the Zion's camp episode deliberately sought to be bitten by a snake, thus to exercise faith and fulfill the promise of the New Testament that if believers should take up any deadly serpent it would not harm them (see Mark 16:18). He was rebuked by the Prophet. The point that emerged was that if, in the line of one's calling, one is in fact bitten, he can expect relief. But one who deliberately seeks it is entitled to no such promise. And so it is, I submit, in all forms of human affliction. Suffering ought to be the by-product of purposeful service, not a self-obsessed way of life.

A second objection, more difficult to remove, is that if this is the purpose of mortality, this coping with opposition, how is it that so few really do triumph? How is it that so many are themselves overcome? Instead of their souls developing, they shrink; instead of their characters being made into steel, they are made into a tormented shambles; instead of taking on the fluids of godliness, they take on the acids of degradation. That is a hard, hard question. It is even harder if we point to innocent suffering. In children's hospitals, for example, some of the patients are well below the age of accountability, with congenital maladies—no arms, no eyes, and many other afflictions that few can bear to see. This is one of the most difficult realities to reconcile with meaning and purpose, and with God's love.

But regardless of purpose, I want to mention three solid facts that are worth remembering. I find them hidden in the Prophet's letter.

The first point is that there are limits to what we can suffer; there is a cut-out point physically and psychically beyond which we lose full alert consciousness. There are kinds of cancer that attack the bone which could persist to unbearable scales of pain except for the fact that there are other organs in the body that, eventually, almost like a fuse, break the circuit. I am among those who are grateful that that is so.

Second, pain does not compound. When it is over, it is over. That's not true of some other kinds of evil, but it's true of pain. Emily Dickinson years ago wrote a poem that fits here. I don't understand the words and yet I understand her. Two lines are indelible. She says: "After great pain, a formal feeling comes. / The nerves sit ceremonious, like tombs." In the next stanza is the phrase, "quartz-like contentment." She is describing the glory of relief. Pain once past does not compound. It is simply over.

Then third, as C. S. Lewis reminds us, it is important to remember that no one is suffering all the pain. We can talk about the fact that if we count right now the number of people in our office or other place of employment, each is suffering a certain amount. We'll call that amount X. If you multiply X by the number of people there are in the world, you come up with four billion X, shall we say. Then add the whole animate creation—the animals, the sparrows, and the insects. William James once said, "This universe will never be all good so long as one cockroach suffers the pangs of unrequited love." Now you have multiple billion X. The Prophet said God desires the happiness of all His creatures. And think of all that pain! But notice: no one is suffering multiple billion X. Each is only suffering his own X.

Only if we could see the outcome, even for the most bitter among us, could we estimate how wise—as well as brave—we were to enter mortality. The miracle is that the same thing—suffering—can have totally opposite effects, depending on how we respond to it.

I know a man who has received 3,200 blood transfusions. He is a hemophiliac, hospitalized with inner bleeding every three weeks. He tells me that each experience is like a "baptismal" . . . "I come out of the hospital feeling like the blackboard has been wiped clean, anxious that it shall not be filled again." He copes with pain with an expression on his face that would convince a child he was praying. He can inspire a depressed soul, whether in the hospital or out. He has not known a day or a night in fifteen years without pain—and I don't mean low-level aches like stiff muscles, pleasant pains. I mean the hydraulic pain of bone joints being forced apart by his own life-giving blood. Some other people I know have suffered far less but are bitter, cynical, hateful.

How can good and bad fruit come from the same experience? The divine and the devilish? It is the root of our spiritual nourishment that changes everything. That is the scale on which we came to be weighed.

Wrote B. H. Roberts, who identified with Joseph Smith as closely as did his blood brothers:

> Some of the lowliest walks in life, the paths which lead into the deepest valleys of sorrow and up to the most rugged steeps of adversity, are the ones which, if a man travel in, will best accomplish the object of his existence in this world. . . . The conditions which place men where they may always walk on the unbroken plain of prosperity and seek for nothing but their own pleasure, are not the best within the gift of God. For in such circumstances men soon drop into a position analogous to the stagnant pool; while those who have to contend with difficulties, brave dangers, endure disappointments, struggle with sorrows, eat the bread of adversity and drink the water of affliction, develop a moral and spiritual strength, together with a purity of life and character, unknown to the heirs of ease and wealth and pleasure. With the English bard, therefore I believe: Sweet are the uses of adversity! (B. H. Roberts, *The Gospel and Man's Relationship to Deity* [Salt Lake City: Deseret Book Co., 1950], pp. 289–90.)

Yes, sweet, but bittersweet. "No chastening for the present seemeth to be joyous, but grievous: nevertheless afterward it yieldeth the peaceable fruit of righteousness unto them which are exercised thereby" (Hebrews 12:11).

As a little boy, I watched a favorite uncle bring in willows with cocoons on them. Later, we saw the slight opening in one and, boy-like, put our ears up against it to hear the seemingly audible groans and strains of the moth. It wanted out. And we wanted to help. We did not ask our wiser uncle. We just found some scissors and with one decisive snip we shed that moth of its confining coat. It lay there, and we waited for it to fly. But it never flew. It quivered and finally died.

The mortal experience will enable us to fly if we will let it, help it, use it with faith in the Christ who "descended below all." The message of the modern prophets, to a man (and none of them, if you look closely, has been spared any of the vicissitudes), is this: that there is meaning and purpose in all things we suffer; that "all these things" can be for our good, however empty and barren they now appear. The elements of truth in the classical theories have been caught up in a greater whole. The Lord is not playing games with us. The outcome will far exceed the price; the "chastening" will be visioned as our blessing, the fiber of soul-quality will leave no regrets, only infinite and eternal gratitude, and the partnership we forged with Him before we entered this refining fire will loom as marvelous to us as does the face of a loving mother in the eyes of a child who has just emerged from his fever . . . healed, alive, and prepared for life, eternal life, life like God's.

The Prophet Joseph Smith declared: "All your losses will be made up to you in the resurrection, provided you continue faithful. By the vision of the Almighty I have seen it." (*Teachings*, p. 296.)

7

THE GOSPEL
AND THE SABBATH

The decision to write on this topic really goes back to many
visits that my wife, Ann, and I have had in the homes of
Orthodox Jewish people—mostly while we were in Israel. We
noted how they observed the Sabbath, especially Shabbat Eve.
That triggered in me a great interest in searching their lore for the
roots of Sabbath observance.

I want to discuss first the origins of these sacred rites, and then
four mighty metaphors. They are more than that to the Jew; they
are mighty meanings of the Sabbath in their lives. Then we'll talk
about startling parallels between what they teach and practice and
what we in the Church teach and practice on this count. Then I'll
share two or three powerful stories about the Sabbath. Then finally, I'll give a description of how the Jews actually bring into
focus these great traditions.

Two cautions at the outset. The Jews do not agree on anything. They, themselves, have a saying: "Two Jews, three opin-
ions." Also, it is important to know that though there is even
today among the Orthodox a most scrupulous observance of the
Sabbath day, they are by no means in the majority, even in Israel.
What I am therefore describing applies to less than a majority in
the contemporary world.

The other caution has to do with our understanding the difficulty the Master had in His own period among the Jews. One of

these difficulties arose from a too strict, too rulish, too self-destroying approach to the Sabbath. He had to say more than once that the Sabbath was made for man, not man for the Sabbath. Yet we can err in supposing that because, as we like to say, that is simply a relic of the law of Moses; we have somehow outgrown it. The truth may be that we are farther down the mountain than they in the full application of what is intended.

Let me start then with a reference to one of the classics in all Jewish literature, by Abraham Joshua Heschel. The title is simply *The Sabbath*. Heschel points out that the origin of the Sabbath is not, as some suppose, the commandment—namely, the fourth—in the Decalogue. It is in the creation narration itself. It is first clear from the records, he points out, that the use of the word *holy* does not occur in the creation narrative for any of the six days of creation. Each of them and what was done, the Lord pronounced to be good.

But on the seventh, and only then, does the word *kaddish*, meaning "holy," occur. There it says God himself sanctified the day. It also suggests, and we have other sources for this view, that somehow God or the gods themselves observe the Sabbath. Observe in the sense of keep, that is. And the commandment "Remember," as in "Remember the Sabbath day," is a Jewish phrase which doesn't exactly mean retain in your memory. It means, more accurately, "memorialize" this day. On the Jewish view (if there is an agreed one), God himself did some creating even on the seventh day. Namely, He created Menohah, which is approximately "tranquility." He left some things behind in terms of labor and creative work, but on the seventh day He created tranquility. Then, say they, so must we.

Some have supposed that to say this day was sanctified or needs to be shows that in the divine plan there is something crucial about time and timing. Does it really matter? The question, of course, is raised most prominently in our generation by the Seventh Day Adventists. Does the exact time one designates for Shabbat really matter? Or does it only matter that in any given series of seven days one be a Sabbath?

Let me point out that we have reason to know that the Lord does care about time and timing. To illustrate this, Doctrine and Covenants section 77 (an interesting number in the present context) clearly teaches that just as there are seven days in our week, which we call twenty-four-hour periods, so in the Lord's economy there are seven one-thousand-year periods. Six of those will constitute the more or less man-controlled history of this earth, but the seventh, as Joseph Smith put it once, will be tried by the Lord himself (see *Teachings*, p. 252).

The Millennium is a day—a one-thousand-year day, following six others of the same duration. If we had unerringly kept the calendar from the beginning, we would know exactly when the Messiah—for us, the Lord Jesus Christ—will come. He will come at the beginning of the seventh thousand-year period. It is expedient that we not know exactly when that is, but it will be then as He has announced.

The Jewish conclusion follows from this sort of reasoning. It is that, far from the Sabbath being a day of strict injunctions, which are joyless duties imposed on duties of the prior day; the Sabbath is the reward for, the outcome of, indeed the climax of all other preparatory creations. It is not an imposed stoppage. It is what all the preparation was designed for, and therefore it has great value. It was, indeed, made for man.

Some have pointed out that even one's ability to work on the six days is enhanced by not working on the seventh. The Jews have a tradition that Moses put that argument to the pharaoh and convinced him; and that therefore the children of Israel in bondage were permitted, on sheer economic grounds, to have one day in seven off. But for mainline Judaism that is beside the real point.

To make a man forget that he is the son of a king, said the Jews, is the worst thing the evil of the universe can achieve. The Sabbath is a day when every man is a king and every woman a queen.

One could argue that the things that might well have destroyed the Jews failed to do so because, if for no other reason, they kept the Sabbath—even in a small degree. They themselves say it isn't the case that the Jews have kept the Sabbath; rather, the Sabbath has kept the Jews. What could have destroyed them? Well, their last prophet, in their own view, was Moses, so they speak of all the others as lesser, and of the end of prophecy. With the loss of a living prophet they lost someone in charge—what we would refer to as a priesthood bearer. No rabbi claims to have the ancient priesthood. They lost their kingdom—they lost the privilege of which David is to them the highest symbol, of having a king who was somehow both a spiritual and a temporal exemplar. They lost their temple—it was destroyed and crushed—and finally even lost their land and were dispersed in a hundred countries in the world. They almost lost their language. How have they survived? Well, many think it is because, even in the dispersion, they have retained this tradition of keeping the Sabbath.

A beautiful myth says that on the Sabbath day, in addition to your own soul, a second soul possesses your body—a good or better soul. And this is a symbolic way of saying that in every man and every woman there are two kinds of inclinations, good and bad. But on the Sabbath, somehow God sees fit to send an extra spirit, if you will, which lifts a man above his ordinary evil inclinations and spells peace.

They also have a story that whenever a Jew returns home from synagogue on Shabbat Eve, two angels follow him—one bad, one good. If when they reach his home all is prepared—the table set, the candles lit—then the good angel prays and says, "May this be the way the Sabbath will be in this home every week." The other angel, against his will, says amen. But if the man returns home and it's just as it always is, more or less in chaos and no effort has been made toward the Sabbath, then the evil angel prays that this may be the way it always is in this home; and the other angel, against his will, says amen.

They go farther in saying that the Sabbath outweighs all other commandments. In some of their literature, to keep the Sabbath is to keep the whole law and to break it is to break the whole law.

I turn now to more on what I call the metaphors. Note that nothing I say will list things you ought to stop doing or start doing on your own Sabbath. What I hope to do is to stir a new attitude, a new feeling, whatever you do. For the Jew, to miss the feeling is to miss it all, and some of us Latter-day Saints are missing it all. Here are four ways in which they teach by metaphor.

First, as I've indicated, they see the Sabbath as a sanctuary in time. Now, it's true they have strict requirements, and even now in Israel there are hospitals which are so prepared, organized, and planned, that they keep the Sabbath. If you care enough, it can be done. But all that discipline—all that "thou shalt not"—is seen as an instrument to joy. A disciplined joy, indeed, but nevertheless

joy and celebration. Mind, says one of the great rabbis, is estab-
lished by joy; by melancholy it is driven into exile. It is a sin, according to Judaism, to be sad on the Sabbath. If that's startling
language, I'll startle you further. The Talmud says that we will be
held personally accountable before the judgment of God for every
legitimate Sabbath pleasure we did not enjoy. We are *commanded*
to have joy. To miss the joy is to miss it all.

This joyous note is marked among them by special things: by
special dress, by a special tablecloth in the evening, by special
food—sumptuous food, in fact. Then there are the twisted loaves.
One tradition says the two loaves wrapped in one symbolize the
word for "remember the Sabbath" and also the word for "keep
the Sabbath." Others say it symbolizes the law and the prophets.
There may be other possibilities, but all point to exhilaration.
Except in certain offshoot groups of Jewish tradition, there is
nothing we can find that is puritanical—if by puritanical we mean
with H. L. Mencken that a Puritan lives in mortal dread that
somewhere, sometime, somebody is enjoying himself. The Jews
talk about the joy of the commandment. This is in their hearts.
This is on their lips. And if I can put it in modern language, they
make a production out of it.

Second, they speak of the Sabbath as a feast. And they remind
themselves over and over that when Moses had the children of
Israel in the wilderness a double portion of manna was given just
before the Sabbath, but none on the Sabbath, so that the day was
recognizable in two ways—by what was absent and what was present. Jews serve the most beautiful meal of the week on Shabbat
Eve. The mother often has to prepare for as much as two days before, and one of the traditional dishes is a kind of stew which stays
simmering all night long the night before the Sabbath and then
needs only to be served. The feast is itself a form of ritual, and it
requires special preparations and special activities. It is, to quote
one writer, a palace in time. Something of the same spirit attends
America's Thanksgiving dinner. It involves, for one thing, the
bringing in of the stranger or of the poor. (This is why Ann and I
had such firsthand and close experiences. We were foreigners, and
were invited for that very reason.) "Come and share our Shabbat."
It is a feast even for the poorest man in the poorest ghetto. Why?
Well, because even if he is poor and cannot afford the twisted

loaves and a little wine and the meat and the fish and the candles, the synagogue in that area will see that he has them. That's a requirement. So on that particular day even a poor man is rich.

The third metaphor has roots in the Jews' mystical tradition, but it has biblical precedent. They talk about the Sabbath as heaven on earth; as—if you want to be specific and mathematical—one-sixtieth of paradise. You have a foretaste of paradise. The seventh day, some legends say, is the reflection of the seventh heaven, the highest heaven. By the way, they also say having dreams is one-sixtieth of being a prophet. They believe that this is cosmic, that nature herself celebrates the Sabbath. In the Church we have a hymn titled "Come Away to the Sunday School." One of the lines is "Nature breathes her sweetest fragrance on the holy Sabbath day." That's the Jews' feeling. Even the rivers don't work on the Sabbath. They are accustomed to throw up rocks and dirt, so they may be very calm on the Sabbath. Even hell celebrates the Sabbath. People who have been tormented in hell are, for purposes of the Sabbath day, released. The hosts of heaven celebrate the Sabbath. They gather and they sing and they feel tranquility.

All the miracles of the six days of creation, say the Jews, are somehow available to us, or should be, on the seventh day. And all creation "resolves itself into melody if we have ears to hear."

Finally, they speak of the Sabbath as a queen, as a bride. How did that get started? Well, here are two traditions. According to Rabbi Simeon, the Sabbath said unto the Holy One (their word for *Adoni*, the Lord) "O master of the universe, every living thing created has its mate, and each day has its companion, except me [this is the Sabbath speaking]. I am alone." The Holy One replied, "Israel will be your mate." So, on their view, Israel cries out to the queen or the bride and says, "Come, holy Sabbath." He who prays on the eve of the Sabbath and recites the verses that begin, "The heavens and the earth were finished"—the scriptures say he is become a partner with the Holy One in creation.

Now, the tradition goes further. The Sabbath is meaningful to God. The world would not be complete if the six days did not culminate at the Sabbath, but they compare this to a king who has made a bridal chamber, has plastered it, painted it, adorned it. Now what does the chamber lack? Obviously, a bride. What did the universe still lack? The Sabbath. Imagine a king who made a ring. What did it lack? A signet. What did the universe lack? A

Sabbath. So the Sabbath is a bride. Its celebration is like a wedding, and the bride is to come lovely and bedecked and perfumed.

There's a subheading to their argument: sanctification. We're taught that the Lord sanctified the Sabbath (Genesis 2:3; Moses 3:3; D&C 77:128); and in Jewish thought, sanctification is associated with marriage. The symbolism is clear. Why do the typical celebrants of the Sabbath among the Hasidic Jews link myrtle with the Sabbath? When going out to invite friends to a wedding, the groom carries myrtle. What is myrtle? Well, the poet Judah Halevi makes the point that *hadas*, the Hebrew word for myrtle, was the original name of Esther, whose beauty was legendary.

An overhead awning of myrtle is erected for the bride during the canopy ceremony of marriage. The old man who in a Jewish story was running at twilight to welcome the Sabbath and carrying two bunches of myrtle was asked why. He's supposed to have replied, "One is for remember and one is for keep." I don't know how close the Greeks are to the Jews on this, but in Greek mythology myrtle was Aphrodite's tree—a special plant and a symbol of love.

On one point there is tremendous overlap. Most traditions about God and creation hold that He did it, finished it, and in effect abandoned it. There was no more creative work for God to do. Sometimes in Jewish parlance, you ask what God has been doing since He finished the creation. They answer, "making marriages." For most Christians, it's all over. Yet Jews speak of continual creation for God. So do we Latter-day Saints, do we not?

Just lift one sentence from the New Testament: "I go to prepare a place for you" (John 14:2). That is further labor. We overlap on the notion that even heaven will involve work, problems, and—dare I say it?—yes, busyness of a kind. It was a great surprise to Wilford Woodruff, in one of his frequent glimpses of the spirit world, to have a conversation with the Prophet Joseph Smith. The Prophet said he was in a hurry. It troubled Elder Woodruff, so he asked the Prophet why. "I expected my hurry would be over when I got [to the Spirit world]." The Prophet explained: "We are the last dispensation and so much work has to be done [to prepare to go to earth with the Savior], and we need to be in a hurry in order to accomplish it." (G. Homer Durham, ed. *The Discourses of Wilford Woodruff* [Salt Lake City: Bookcraft, 1969], pp. 288–89.) Yet there is a kind of rest—peace and joy—

that can occur even in the midst of such concern. Hence the one kind of work that Orthodox Jewry will permit its rabbis to do on the Sabbath is work for God. None other.

On the idea of the Sabbath as bride, I have a letter from a friend—a Jewish mother—who visited my wife and me and mentioned that she'd had chats with the rabbi out of the campaigns for what a woman should or should not be doing, and that she'd been completely satisfied with what he taught her. So I asked her, "What does it mean in your tradition for the woman to be the queen of the Sabbath?" Here are a few sentences from her reply. "The mother is responsible for the atmosphere of piety and reverence and for the teaching of Jewish ideals. She prepares the Shabbat dinner" (by the way, the men are encouraged to help and we've seen them do it), "and gathers her children around while she pronounces the blessing over the lights. The woman prepares the home for each festival. She creates the mood of joy. She is general counselor. The Talmud says no matter how short your wife is, lean down and take her advice. And for husbands—another Talmudic statement—but how can a man be assured of having a blessed home? Answer: By respecting his wife." (I love all these old sayings, subtle stories, and yiddish theater.) Then she goes on. "The woman sets the spiritual tone. She is the most responsible for her children. It is an enormous responsibility and a joy to have." Well, that's from a Jewish mother. The Jewish mother has great influence and power in the home.

Now I shift to some parallels. Be honest about the kinds of predicament we frequently are in when the Sabbath begins, and you can ask how anyone can really let go wholeheartedly. We have read together, Ann and I, a famous novel by Herman Wouk, *The Caine Mutiny*, and more recently his two books which have been compared to Tolstoy, *War and Remembrance* and *The Winds of War*. Herman Wouk is a playwright and therefore on Friday has often been in that situation which characterizes Broadway opening plays—rehearsals; the play tottering toward probable disaster, and so on. But at the first sign of a star (the Jewish Sabbath begins when you can see two stars in the evening) he abandons his play and as an Orthodox Jew goes home, where he finds his children (whom he hasn't been noticing lately) in their best bib and tucker, finds his wife with everything prepared. He describes it as like coming home from the wars. He knows that from sundown to sundown it is "time out," and no one who respects him can get to him—the telephone is off, so is the television; nothing mechanical is supposed to be utilized in a strict Orthodox home. One of his friends, a producer, said to him one day after this had been repeated many times, "I do not envy you your religion, but I do envy you your Sabbath."

Let's consider some of the pressures that are upon us just as we enter the Sabbath, and show how both Judaism and, I suggest, Mormonism have a response. Suppose you are poor. Well, as I've said, in Judaism the poor are invited in, and if they lack, they are provided with the essentials of Sabbath devotion. In several places in the Doctrine and Covenants, Latter-day Saints are taught not to be so concerned about riches per se. "He that hath eternal life is rich. Seek not for riches but for wisdom." (D&C 6:7; 11:7.) The Sabbath is the day when wisdom can be reenthroned. Suppose you have failed or had setbacks during the week. The Jewish teaching is that the Sabbath will renew your perspective, and your failure will seem somewhat trivial in relationship to the ultimate plans and purposes and promises of God.

But suppose you are sinful. Judaism says that the Sabbath is not a day for confession and for mourning.

There we split a little. We have in section 59 of the Doctrine and Covenants a commandment—the whole section has the flavor of Sabbath observance—to confess our sins one to another and before the Lord. That has come to mean not detailing our actual transgressions, but the acknowledgment of need, and that we are sinful (and just by coming to church we acknowledge it). Well, presumably if you are mourning for your own sins or for the loss of a loved one you should keep that private on Sunday, because you are to have a glad heart on that day. We are so commanded. If we do this, says section 59, "with a glad heart and a cheerful countenance—not with much laughter, for this is sin—but with a glad heart," then are the promises fulfilled. I know people who have occasionally tried to impress others with how sad they look because they have fasted all that time, but our revelation says that fasting and prayer are "rejoicing and prayer." That comes as news to most children. But the intent is the same, I believe, as the Jewish intent that fasting ought to be feasting on the Spirit. Going without food combined with a prayerful heart is supposed to contribute to that kind of feasting. It it doesn't, you have missed the joy and have missed it all.

But suppose you are condemned. Well, in their tradition you're out of prison for that day, and even in prison the glory can surround you. But suppose your soul is itself deeply wounded. Join the club. We're commanded to come to church with a broken heart and a contrite spirit. If you trace the roots of that phrase, you will find they are, in one word, "buffeted." Come, acknowledging it if you've been beaten down this week. You always have, but if you'll come with a proper spirit you will be healed and renourished.

But suppose you are rushed, and there are projects and pressures and commitments and so on. The Jewish view is to stop, slow down, be quiet, and you'll have greater strength to carry on. Our version of that—it's also an Old Testament phrase—is "Be still and know that I am God" (D&C 101:16). We can't really know that when the din is as strong in our ears as it usually is. I sometimes think that the very volume of some contemporary music—and I hesitate to use the word *music* for what I'm describing—is exactly designed to quiet and muffle the scream of our inner world and our life and conscience. As if we could drown it out with the noise.

But suppose we are at war? In Jewish thinking, war justifies bending the Sabbath. The Jews have been taken advantage of occasionally by enemies who said: "Ah-ha! we know how to get to the Jews. We'll attack, and they won't fight on Shabbat." So they do fight. And they do fight if necessary on Yom Kippur, as the Egyptians found out some years ago. But their commitment arises from the conviction that there are emergencies. Nevertheless, much of their Sabbath celebration, in the past, has been in the midst of crisis. Ann and I have been to Israel many times. Hardly a time, prior to the time we departed, have we not been counseled by friends: "Don't go! This is the worst possible time. There's a crisis over there." Of course, they're always right. In Israel they live in the midst of such crisis, but they keep the Sabbath. It would not be wrong to say they keep it precisely in part because it is a crisis world in which they live, and on the Sabbath they close out that world—the jungle, the bombs, the guns. They pull the drapes and it is not proper to talk about war or politics, even to think about them, during the time of rejoicing.

But suppose all of your machines have broken down? The mechanical ox is in the mire? Well, one of the blessings they claim of the Sabbath is that you get back to the simple elements of life for God's earth as it is and for the most elemental way of living.

What if you are filled with anger? Their answer: You shall kindle no fire, and that, of course, is literal fire; but they go on, not even the fire of righteous indignation. Peace. And so we have been counseled, "Renounce war and proclaim peace" (D&C 98:16), especially on the day of peace.

But suppose you are bitter and unforgiving. Come to the sweets and taste and forgive. We have done that as a church. There is a jubilee year in traditional Jewry when whoever is imprisoned or has debts and so on is forgiven and released. By the way, no interest is charged on the Sabbath in strict Jewish reckoning.

But what if your animals are in need? Their answer is, let them rest.

An offshoot group, not strictly the Orthodox, going back to the fifteenth century are convinced that joy is the giant cure-all; that if you can be enthusiastically happy, then all evils somehow are walked under your feet. If you can't, then no other solution will ultimately do. Two men from this group were arguing about who was the greatest miracle worker among the rabbis, and one of them had a rabbi who, he thought, qualified. This rabbi was going along a highway when a storm gathered. He had clothing on that he wanted preserved, and also he didn't want to drown; so by use of his great power he caused that, though there was rain to the right of him and rain to the left of him, where he was traveling there was no rain.

The other man was not impressed. "That's nothing," he said. "My rabbi was on the way to a distant town on Friday, which he thought he could reach before sundown (when the Sabbath began). But the driver had miscalculated, and now, suddenly, dusk was falling. He saw he was in danger, God forbid, of violating the Sabbath; whereupon, he performed his miracle. He put forth his hands, and behold it was Sabbath to the right of him and Sabbath to the left of him, but in the center there was no Sabbath—it was the middle of the week."

A second story: A poor man was the Sabbath guest of a rich one. He ate so voraciously and with such vigor that perspiration streamed down his face. "My friend," said his host, "why do you work so hard?" "Because," he replied, "I'm trying to fulfill the commandment 'in the sweat of thy face shalt thou eat thy bread.'"

Then there is the delightful story of a maker of books whose name, allegorically, was Shabbati. His family and he were so poor that they did not have anything for the Sabbath, but they were too proud to go to their neighbors, who would have been under obligation either to invite them or to provide them with the essentials. He went home late from the synagogue so nobody could even inquire of his situation.

When he arrived home, there was the Sabbath table fully prepared—everything in order; the candles lighted, and his wife looking fresh and delightful. How did it happen? Well, his wife had found an old garment and also some gold buttons. She had hastened to the market and turned in the buttons for their worth in money and had prepared the Sabbath meal. He was so delighted at this that he took his wife in his arms. (This is how he reported it in confessing to his rabbi). "Master, I could not contain myself. Tears fell from my eyes. I praised the Lord. I praised Him again and again. We began to sing. I forgot the majesty of the Sabbath. I took my wife by the hand, led her out, and we danced in our little house. Then we sat down to eat, but I was so overcome with the fish course that I jumped up, took her in my arms, and danced again. Then we ate the soup. I danced a third time, and cried for happiness. But oh, Master, it came to me afterwards that perhaps our dancing and laughter had disturbed the sublimity of God's Sabbath. If we have sinned, we have come to ask for penance."

What did the rabbi reply? "Know that all the hierarchy of heaven sang and laughed and was joyful and danced hand in hand with this aged man and his wife when they were happy on the Sabbath Eve. And when you heard my laughter"—the rabbi had laughed three times himself, to the great shock of many—"it was because I was with them in spirit when they went out to dance, and I danced and sang with them."

That's not a Puritan Sabbath. But you may find such celebration and rejoicing in the Nauvoo period of Mormon history.

Now finally, how is it done in practice? Ann and I were invited into many Jewish homes, and I'll give you a description that's mostly of one home. Let me just say as the preface that most of the Christian writers I have read tend to suppose that heaven is an effortless place, and usually their descriptions of hell are far more interesting. But these persons we visited had put in great labor and preparation to make the Sabbath a creative experience. In the home of an Orthodox rabbi who had four lovely daughters and whose synagogue we had earlier attended, we saw the essential components—his wife, his children, the lights, the twisted loaves, the meat, and the *gefilt*, fish. We saw the *kipah* or *kipot* (the latter would be the plural). These are the little skull caps, which an Orthodox Jew wears everywhere but which others wear in synagogue and on sacred occasions. We were given our own. If it seems strange to you that a person would cover his head in reverence rather than uncover it, just think a little more deeply about your own experience in the temple.

After the evening had come—the two stars could be seen—we witnessed the tablecloth, the beautiful *chollah*. We learned that there had been a ritual bath for some family members, not just a usual bath but a Shabbat bath. We listened to their songs. Some do not sing well, but they make a joyful noise. We thought we could detect certain overtones of Russian music and Eastern European music, and that's understandable because the majority who escaped the Holocaust and came to Israel have such roots. It sounded almost like a Russian cossack chorus. Their music is the kind that leads you to respond to the rhythm, to clap, to motion. For them the ultimate outcome of good music is dance. We witnessed the prayers, the ceremonial lighting of the candles (in one other home we attended, they sang a transition hymn that starts on a worldly level and then moves into a reverent attitude). We partook of each of the cups of wine, which in our case was grape juice. This has to be a product of the vine, but it can be raisin juice or grape juice or wine—any of the three. With each of these came a certain ceremonial prayer.

As he broke the bread, the father, who was also a rabbi, handed it to us. You have to somehow be in touch as he is in touch. We saw the use of the ritual salt, based on Leviticus— "With all thine offerings thou shalt offer salt." We saw how very congenial was the discussion between parents and children. It's the children's day; they know they have their parents on this day, if on no other. On this particular evening we did not hear the reading of Proverbs 31, but in another home we did, and that's often a ritual—the famous verses about who can find a virtuous woman, who is more precious than rubies. In one home I was asked to read that, and in the presence of the woman to whom these passages were applied I was moved more than I can describe. There are Jewish mothers, I'm told, who resent the reading of those words because they think it is sop, as it were, of comfort after neglect and hostility all week; then suddenly the husband waxes poetic and gives them their just due.

There is an intimacy we observed even in their feeling for the divine, though they're very careful, out of long philosophical tradition, to keep God distant. And yet some rabbis do not feel bad about referring to God as Daddy; and they're not talking about big daddy or Daddy Warbucks. It's a matter of the intimate warmth of filial love. In one home we witnessed a blessing pronounced upon the youngest son, and this is also ceremonial and traditional. And the blessings were of *Ephraim* and *Manasseh*. Latter-day Saints will recognize that. The blessings of Ephraim and Manasseh! A Jew pronouncing such a blessing upon his youngest son or grandson? Yes. That's a tradition.

In one home we heard the hymn that is used at the end of the Sabbath, on Saturday night. It's a prayer for the immediate return of Elijah. Their tradition is that Elijah can't come on Friday because everybody's too busy preparing for the Sabbath. He can't come on the Sabbath because that's a day of rest. But the tradition is that he will come on the day after Shabbat. Just for interest, if you'll read Doctrine and Covenants section 110 and check the date you'll find it was April 3, 1836, when Elijah came to the Kirtland Temple. That was a Passover Sunday, the day after the Jewish Shabbat.

At the end of the day, the Jews have a little ceremony—you taste something special, you smell something special. And now the Sabbath queen leaves and you're back to the work week.

All this moved us. Through the warp and weft of my comments you see that there's a creative idea here—an act of creation is involved in making the Sabbath what the Sabbath ought to be. If a person doesn't do this, for him the day is not a Sabbath at all. Also, through what I've described, there emerges a balance of solemnity on the one hand and pleasure on the other—even very worldly pleasure, if you want to say it that way. Should we be embarrassed by that or troubled by it? Not, I think, if you read section 59, which promises not only blessings from above and revelations in their time—which you would expect from Sabbath observance—but also, on the condition that we do it in rejoicing, very earthly blessings. The promise, precisely worded, is "the fulness of the earth is yours." It names houses, gardens, barns, orchards, vineyards. Those are all temporal, down-to-earth realities. And then the senses—to strengthen the body, to enliven the soul, to please the eye, to gladden the heart, for taste and for smell, and so forth. All these are physical, yet they have spiritual counterparts. The wholeness of Sabbath worship is holness. It involves all of man—body and spirit—and that insight is in authentic Judaism.

It's not uncommon among us, I'm afraid, to think of the Sabbath in a negative way, as a set of tough requirements—perhaps to avoid desecrating it. What I would hope has emerged here is the other side—the beautiful, joyful, happiness-giving effect of sanctifying the day as partners with the Creator. I think it is common to think that if we don't do certain things, there will be positive rewards—that we will be rewarded for sacrifice, for suffering, for service—but very uncommon to think that God will reward us for rejoicing, for enjoying, and for feeling pleasure. The Jewish tradition is, I repeat, that God will in fact reward and compound the very pleasures of the Sabbath. Otherwise it would be as if, beaten and tattered, invited in from afar to a magnificent feast, one refuses to partake of it.

A parable puts it thus: A man who has earned seven coins and is carrying them along the streets sees a poor beggar and out of compassion gives him six coins. Then as he continues walking down the street, he discovers that the beggar has followed him and stolen the seventh one. God has given us six days for labor. It is a terrible mistake to steal the seventh day, which is both His and ours—the very climax and meaning of what has gone before.

I submit that the Sabbath is a time whose idea has come.

8

THE AWESOME POWER OF MARRIED LOVE

These days we see around us an increasing disintegration not only of such family solidarity as once existed, but even in the rejection of the idea of family. Articles are published that say the family is long gone. It is outmoded. But it is interesting to contemplate this fact: that though divorce has never been more frequent, remarriage has never been more frequent; and that people who have struggled and felt that they have failed, and have been estranged and divorced, are trying again and again, suggesting that for all the propaganda to the contrary there is a strong, lasting thirst for the fulfillments that marriage promised. And I am convinced that in the Church—though there is so much anguish and in many marriages struggle—we at least have a greater vision of the possibilities and a greater set of helps to reach toward them than any people in the world.

Now the opening question: What is love? "The awesome power of love" is a phrase from an anthropologist named Ashley Montague. He tells of an orphanage, a foundling home in New York, where orphaned children were taken. Their mortality rate— just the sheer life-and-death struggle—was appalling; two out of three died before the end of the first year.

But then a flourishing contrast was noticed in one particular section of the orphanage: none of the children there seemed to have the struggles to live that the others did. And so, as scientists will, the authorities began various sorts of observation, asking themselves questions as they went along. What could be the reason? Were they eating something different? Were they getting a different kind of nurturing? What was the story?

Well, by accident, which often happens in science (they call it serendipity) they discovered the explanation. There was on that particular wing of the orphanage-hospital a scrub woman whom everyone knew as Old Anna. Her task was to clean the floors. She was as big as a streetcar, but she loved little children. Though she had been forbidden to do it, when no one was looking she would pick them up and hold them. She would sometimes even strap them two at a time on her big hips, and then as she worked on the floor she would lean over and talk to them. She loved them. Those children lived. They ate more. They slept better. They were healthier. And the mortality rate in that wing was well down.

The next question was how to clone Old Anna. They couldn't, of course. But this story underlines that love, whatever it is, is powerful. And after much reading and much talking with knowledgeable people, I have concluded that Paul's definition is the one that does the most to help us understand the nature of love—it is a "fruit of the Spirit" (Galatians 5:22). But I would even go so far as to say that love is the Spirit; that the very love that God has for us is manifested most powerfully through the Spirit. I have always believed this, but let me share by paraphrase something that says it better than I could.

Elder Parley P. Pratt describes the effect of his spending several days with the Prophet in Philadelphia, which is, interestingly, the City of Love. He says the Prophet "lifted a corner of the veil and [gave] me a single glance into eternity."

During these days, Elder Pratt recorded, "[the Prophet] taught me many great and glorious principles. . . . I received from him the first idea of eternal family organization. . . . It was from him that I learned that the wife of my bosom might be secured to me for time and all eternity; and that the refined sympathies and affections which endeared us to each other emanated from the fountain of divine eternal love." (*Autobiography of Parley P. Pratt* [Salt Lake City: Deseret Book Co., 1938], p. 297.)

In clarifying this important subject, the Prophet in effect inverted everything Parley P. Pratt and other early converts had believed about marriage and family when they joined the Church. That the Fall, for example, was really Eve's betrayal of Adam. That's a standard view still in the wider Christian world. This erroneous concept labels women as inferior. That's just for openers. They also believed that the body, being matter, was intrinsically evil, so using two bodies in the procreative act, using them as instruments, had to be wrong—in any case an embarrassment. Why hadn't God arranged it so that children could be brought into the world in some other way? Third, there was the belief that marriage was of the earth, earthy, and perhaps a compromise with the devil. And finally, in the life to come all earthly marriage relationships would be done away.

What Joseph Smith did was to invert or turn around, not just contradict, all four of those. Number one, the Fall was in fact a knowing and *wise* decision of both Eve and Adam in order to make possible the very conditions that would build and perpetuate family. Number two, the body is not intrinsically evil, but is— and this is one of the most sacred words in our vocabulary—a temple. Yes, it can be abused and distorted, but as God intends it to be, it can be glorified and hallowed.

Third, marriage, far from being a compromise of the world and of the devil, is properly the highest ordinance of the kingdom of God, reserved for the highest sanctuary room in the temple— the sealing room. And finally, far from its all being done away hereafter, only for the righteous and the sanctified will the privilege of everlasting marriage and family be granted. The others will be the lonely and the estranged, at least in the full sense of their possibilities. Having been taught by the Prophet, Parley P. Pratt wrote: "I had loved before, but I knew not why. . . . I could now love with the spirit and with the understanding also." That is the blessing of the Restoration. If we can only begin to glimpse that, it gives us the bearings upon which to shape our course.

On one occasion Brigham Young was approached by two women who were asking for a divorce, and he gave an idealistic response. He said to them: "If that dissatisfied wife would behold the transcendent beauty of person, the Godlike qualities of the resurrected husband she now despises, her love for him would be unbounded and unutterable. Instead of despising him, she would feel like worshipping him. He is so holy, so pure, so perfect, so filled with God in his resurrected body. There will be no dissatisfaction of this kind in the resurrection of the just. The faithful elders will have then proved themselves worthy of their wives, and are prepared then to be crowned gods, to be filled with all the attributes of the gods that dwell in eternity. Could the dissatisfied ones see a vision of the future glorified state of their husbands, love for them would immediately spring up within you, and no circumstance could prevail upon you to forsake them." (Church Historical Department document Ms/d/1234 box 49/FD8.) Now, it also works the other way around, that if the husband could only see his wife in her glorified condition, he would be so moved he would feel to worship. You might pause and say, "Wait, wait, wait. We are talking idolatry. We are not supposed to worship each other." In the ultimate scheme of things we will feel to do so when the person is worthy of it.

But Brother Brigham was also practical—he had one foot in this world and one in the next. It is said that a woman came to him one day and said, "Brother Brigham, my husband told me to go to hell," and Brigham said, "Sister, don't go."

We live in a world where there is much clamor and struggle and anguish respecting the role of woman. I heard of a man who literally dragged his wife, I mean bodily dragged her, into a stake president's office, sat her down, and said, "Now, President So-and-So, you tell my wife to honor my priesthood, and then our problems will be solved." This good stake president had his scriptures ready. He opened them to Doctrine and Covenants section 121, verse 37, and said, "Brother, according to what I read here, you have no priesthood."

Elder James E. Talmage wrote: "In the restored Church of Jesus Christ, the Holy Priesthood is conferred, as an individual bestowal, upon men only, and this in accordance with Divine requirement. It is not given to woman to exercise the authority of the Priesthood independently; nevertheless, in the sacred endowments associated with the ordinances pertaining to the House of the Lord, woman shares with man the blessings of the Priesthood. When the frailties and imperfections of mortality are left behind, in the glorified state of the blessed hereafter, husband and wife will administer in their respective stations, seeing and understanding alike"—oh, hasten the day!—"and co-operating to the full in the government of their family kingdom. Then shall woman be recompensed in rich measure for all the injustice that womanhood has endured in mortality. Then shall woman reign by Divine right, a queen in the resplendent realm of her glorified state, even as exalted man shall stand, priest and king unto the Most High God." And then he adds in full confirmation of what Brother Brigham said: "Mortal eye cannot see nor mind comprehend the beauty, glory, and majesty of a righteous woman made perfect in the celestial kingdom of God." (In *Young Woman's Journal*, October 1914, pp. 602–3.)

Now, some are going to say, "I don't quite understand, because we are taught, aren't we, that the spirit we leave this life with we will have in the next life, and everything we take there by the way of failure and sin is going to be perpetuated. So what you're saying sounds like it's sort of a magical cure-all."

This quotation does not say that it is all automatic. According to Elder Bruce R. McConkie there is a fallacy in the Church, and that is that in order for us to be worthy of a celestial resurrection we must be perfect before we leave this life. It is false. While each of us is expected to make all the progress possible in mortality, we cannot be fully perfected in this world. There will be more to be done in the spirit world, but in the glorious celestial resurrection much improvement will take place. And that vision—that really it is going to happen and if we live consistently it will happen—can make a lot of difference during the hours of discouragement and despair. There are problems in some marriages and in some families that will not all be resolved here, and it is pointless to hope that they will. But it is not pointless to have long-range faith that as you continue doing your all, they will be resolved, and that's the promise that these prophets have given us.

Latter-day Saints who have really embarked in the service of God have a celestial homesickness. The words of the hymn "O My Father" turn out to be the most requested words of all the mail that has ever come to Temple Square in Salt Lake City. Even in the secular world—people out there who have never heard of the understanding of the family that we have—even they sense in those words something poignantly nostalgic, "Father, Mother, let me come and dwell with thee." Eliza R. Snow wrote the words to this hymn, of course. Zina Diantha Huntington, who at age eighteen lost her mother under very trying circumstances in Nauvoo, went to the Prophet and expressed an ultimate concern: "Will I know my mother as my mother when I get over on the other side?" And the Prophet replied: "Certainly you will. More than that, you will meet and become acquainted with your eternal Mother, the wife of your Father in Heaven." Such an idea had never entered her head, and she burst out, "And have I, then, a Mother in Heaven?" He replied: "You assuredly have. How could a Father claim His title unless there were also a Mother to share that parenthood?" The record continues: "It was about this time that Sister Snow learned the same glorious truth from the same inspired lips, and at once she was moved to express her own great joy and gratitude in the moving words of the hymn, 'O My Father.'" (Recollection of Susa Young Gates, in *History of the Young Ladies MIA* [Salt Lake City: *Deseret News*, 1911], p. 16.)

We don't know how extensive and detailed the organization of the family was in the premortal life, but we were family there. We *were a family*. And according to George Q. Cannon (see *Utah Genealogical and Historical Magazine* 21:124) and Orson F. Whitney (see *Improvement Era* 13:100–1), who gave this a lot of thought, it may well be that some of the kinships we feel for each other here are but the trailing of the impressions and expressions of those former associations.

I once had the opportunity to ask a related question to Elder Joseph Fielding Smith. I was at the Church offices doing some research when I ran into his wife. Since she was going into his office, which was then in the Historical Department, she took me with her. "Let's go see Daddy," she said. I knew who Daddy was. As the great Church scripturalist, he overawed me. He looked up with a smile and said, "Brother Madsen, you can have one question." So I asked, "Brother Smith, do you think marriages are made in heaven?" Well, I had him over a barrel—his wife was standing right there. And he hesitated, so she kind of punched him. "Daddy, Daddy, don't you think our marriage was made in heaven?" Now, he had to be honest. So he said, "Well, it's in heaven now."

The Church has never given sanction to the idea that somehow all Latter-day Saint marriages were predetermined in heaven, but there is an interesting Jewish tradition that answers the question "What has God been doing since the creation?" with "Making marriages."

In this church we know, as others in the religious world don't know, that we didn't begin our existence or our family consciousness in this world.

Many of us have heard the statement made—and ascribed to either Joseph Smith or Brigham Young—to the effect that if a person could see the glory of the telestial kingdom he would commit suicide to get there. If only we could get the fundamental doctrines across to Church members as rapidly as we get across rumors, everyone would be saved. Am I saying that's a rumor? Well, I am saying this, that over a period of many years I have combed everything Joseph Smith said and wrote, and I can't find it. Hugh Nibley has done the same with Brigham Young's words, and he can't find it. It is hard to prove a negative, of course. What I can say is that we have found a statement from Joseph via Wilford Woodruff that says something else that is close, and I suspect it is the origin of the alleged statement (see *Diary of Charles C. Walker*, August 1837, in Church Historical Department). Elder Woodruff said the Prophet taught this, roughly: that if we could see what is beyond the veil we couldn't stand to stay here in mortality for five minutes. And I suggest from the context that he was not talking about the telestial kingdom. He was talking about what it was like to be in the presence of God and the family.

Speaking of homesickness, the Lord's anesthesia is our amnesia. We would not stand this operation except for the fact that the curtain has been drawn over our past. So we do not know our name and rank and serial number. We have no specific memories of our premortal lives. Patriarchs give us a glimpse under inspiration. We have forgotten so we will stay here and tough out the spook alley. That is not a bad metaphor, because there was complete understanding before we got into this tunnel of why and what it would lead to. That's why we had the courage to shout for joy at the prospect (see Job 39:7), which in light of present circumstances is astonishing. We were able to envision what it could lead to because there we were in the presence of it. We would come back, should we be so blessed, and be like our Father and our Mother.

For some years now I have been much involved in studying Jewish lore, and for a semester I taught at Haifa University. It has been exciting to find specific instances of the fact that we in the Church have much in common with the great mainstream tradition of Judaism respecting the family. The Jews speak of some kind of premortal arrangements. They speak of the fall of man in positive terms, as we do. Yes, it brought bitter conditions, but as the language of Genesis says, the curse is "for [our] sake" (3:17). And yes, we have the promise of difficulty and pain in childbirth, but says the promise, "they shall be saved in child-bearing" (JST 1 Timothy 2:15). Not easy, but fruitful.

Further, the Jews say that somehow Adam was originally two bodies, and the Lord took off one to make Eve. They say that Abraham was promised above all else that he would have a posterity that was not just as numerous as the stars but also would shine like the stars—not just quantity but quality too. Abraham's willingness to go on Mount Moriah and offer his only son—they call that the *akeda*. That means the binding. Their legend says that Isaac asked to be bound, so that he would not involuntarily prevent his father from sinking a knife. They say that Abraham's and Isaac's response was the greatest willingness and sacrifice in history, and therefore the place which had been flat before became a mountain after; God exalted the place. They say that Sarah didn't date her life until after the birth of Isaac. They say that every line in her face disappeared after Isaac was born. They say that the reason why murder is so wrong is that it destroys not just a life but a race. They say that the notion that somehow marriage is against the will of God is contrary to the truth; that getting married is one of the chief things God wants us to do, and that the heavens rejoice over a marriage where there is a genuine exchange of love. Finally, in their traditions, it is not inappropriate to call the Lord what I mentioned Jesse Evans called her husband—not just Father, but Daddy. That's what *Abba* means in Hebrew.

Well, some of that has echoes in our hearts. Yet I was quoting not from Mormon sources but Jewish ones.

Now, one other glimpse far beyond in an exchange of letters between Heber C. Kimball and his wife, Vilate, that reflects love at their mature level, after they had been through all that occurred from New York to Nauvoo. She was writing to him while he was away on the next to last of his several missions. (It is a paradox that this marvelous church that is so inclined to glorify and celebrate family has often required that members leave the immediate family to go and serve the wider family.) She wrote in part: "Let your heart be comforted, and if you never more behold my face in time, let this be my last covenant and testimony unto you: that I am yours in time and throughout all eternity. This blessing has been sealed upon us by the Holy Spirit of promise, and cannot be broken only through transgression, or committing a grosser crime than your heart or mine is capable of."

Heber was so moved that he wrote a reply which became a prayer. It asked that they could live together and die together because, said he, "Thou, O God, knowest we love each other with pure hearts." (*Life of Heber C. Kimball*, pp. 334–35.)

The last prophecy Heber C. Kimball uttered was made as he walked along behind Vilate's casket and said, "I shall not be long after her." And he wasn't.

One of the consequences of such unifying love under the power of the Holy Spirit is that it makes separation almost like amputation. Yet in the vision of what ultimately can be and will be, and in the knowledge that there is yet to be some relationship in the spirit world, we can abide here in love and hope.

President Spencer W. Kimball, himself a great example in this matter, taught the Church much. Let me say that I once sat with him in a ticklish situation of marriage counseling. He drew two overlapping figures that were somewhat like circles, but the overlap in the center was a larger area than the two ends that didn't overlap. And his point was that differences—man, woman, husband, wife—maybe are no-man's-lands or no-woman's-lands. These he and Camilla just never entered and learned not to try to. We should acknowledge that. That's an individual problem. Perhaps it will be resolved eventually, but when you find out that there are some areas in which you just are not overlapping, then endure them.

For example, I know a man who insists on making pancakes on Saturday morning. Maybe his wife wants to suggest the proper bowl, and perhaps a little less flour, or some other idea that might improve the pancakes. He almost drives her out with a hatchet. "Now, now—this is mine!" So she has learned to just sleep a little longer and then come down and eat the pancakes. That's a non-overlap area.

On the other hand, in every marriage there are happy places where the two overlap, and those are to be cherished.

President Kimball enunciated three principles in this connection. One is *humor*. *Forgiveness* is next—a hard one. And he also talked a lot about coping and overcoming selfishness, about developing *unselfishness!* He said that giant strides could be made in most households if we would really cultivate these three qualities.

First, then, humor. It is one of the most powerful ways of stimulating thinking. Think of that. But that's not the reason why I am recommending it. I am recommending it as the oil that smooths the frictions of life, and especially in the home. I am not talking about the humor that portrays something sacred. We have been warned against that. If you laugh at sacred things, make light of them, you will lose the Spirit. I am talking about the humor that laughs at oneself, that acknowledges one's foibles and finds them funny instead of tragic.

One of the best examples I know is President Hugh B. Brown, to whom I was close in his last years. His dear wife was post-stroke paralyzed in those years and at the final stages could not even speak. They had a nurse in the home during the last year or so. One day in his late eighties, after taking a bath (his annual bath, he jested) President Brown climbed out and began to work on the ring around the tub. Suddenly he got a stitch in his back; he couldn't stand up. Problem: Should he call the nurse? He tried several things. Nothing worked. And then it occurred to him that if he crawled on his hands and knees, he could perhaps roll onto the bed. So he started crawling. As he did so, it became clear to him what he might look like from the point of view of a spectator. He started to laugh, and that made his back hurt more. Now, I suppose that you could tell that story and get people to weep if you left out the humor. They would see it as a tragic situation— that *poor old man*. But he handled it with humor.

He was sometimes delightfully clever even in those late years. On one occasion Elder Boyd K. Packer took him by the arm as he was struggling with those bad legs. "Brother Brown, can I be your cane?" He replied quickly, "Yes, if I am Abel."

He was walking down the aisle with an aged sister when she said, "Oh, President Brown, I have always wanted you to speak at my funeral." He responded, "Sister, if you want me to speak at your funeral, you'd better hurry."

Some might think: Wait a minute; can a person laugh about something as serious as death? Yes. There he was in bed (this really happened, his daughter told me the story); he had had a kind of stroke, and the doctor summoned the family, suggesting that he probably wouldn't make it through the night. So there they were gathered solemnly around his bed. But at about 5:00 A.M. he started to rally. He got better! Still better! Finally he opened an eye, only one, and he surveyed the situation. They saw a slight curl on his lip, and he said, "I fooled you, didn't I?"

What's wrong with that? Nothing, that is *joie de vivre*, and only one who has spirituality and vision can have that kind of sweet, self-deprecating humor.

Let me say to the men, instead of getting rigid and defensive when you've made a foolish mistake, laugh at yourself, acknowledge it. Your wife will agree with you. It's wholesome. It blows the pretenses away. It cleans out the carburetor in your life. You laugh with each other. I am not talking about pointing a finger at her and laughing at her. That's wrong. Don't do that in public or in private. But laugh at yourself.

We all catch ourselves in stupidities at times. They occur frequently in my house. My children all know that I am supposed to be able to put a lecture together, but nevertheless I make language mistakes. Sometimes I fluff a whole line—really mess it up. For instance, "The queen showed up with a twenty-one-sun galute and wore her gownless evening strap." So my daughter always says, "All right, Dad, get out of that one," and then I try. They know what's going on, and they laugh and then I laugh. And of course, that lubricates. Now, in our families we need more of it. Is that compatible with spirituality? It is, and maybe good, clean humor and true spirituality require each other.

Let me suggest an even closer example of this. I wish I knew it was true. It's an apocryphal story, I'm afraid, but I want it to be true. It goes as follows: A young man goes one day to see Elder Harold B. Lee when he is President of the Church. He walks in and solemnly announces: "I have had a revelation for the Church, and I am here to tell it to you so you will tell the Church. It is that the Church is mistaken in asking converts to wait a year before receiving the temple endowment. Now you know." How would you handle that if you were the President? In our story, President Lee says: "I am not going to question your religious experience, but I have noticed something since you came in. You haven't smiled once. And anyone who takes himself that seriously is not likely to be receiving much revelation."

Think about it. It is the case that humor enables us to have a proper perspective and to acknowledge our finitudes and our failures and get past them. But being rigid and solemn and unyielding—that is the way to a dreary life and an early grave.

Elder LeGrand Richards was proof of what I am saying. The man's face was almost frozen in a smile before he was gone. What a delightful human being! Somebody asked him how he accounted for his longevity. (By the way, he attended the fiftieth wedding anniversary of his daughter. Figure that out. "Why don't we invite the folks over for our fiftieth wedding anniversary?") "Brother Richards, how have you managed to live so long?" He said, "I've never worried." Think of that. We all worry. Some people don't worry because they just don't know what's going on. Elder Richards didn't worry because he *did* know what was going on. Testimony, faith, insight, prophetic glimpses—he could cope, therefore, in ways that others couldn't, and he laughed at himself. Delightful! So cultivate humor; restore it to your home if it's been lost.

About forgiveness. A tough line from the Doctrine and Covenants talks about patiently bearing attacks from one's enemies (see D&C 98:23–24). You say: "Wait a minute, we're talking about the home. We don't have any enemies at home." Is that so? Sometimes our hardest struggles to eliminate friction are with the people we love or are trying to love. And though the revelation was given in the context of the brutal persecutions the Saints endured during the Missouri period, surely the spirit of it must carry over to all situations of potential hostility. Bear it patiently, the scripture says, even if the person who is hurting you hasn't shown the first sign of repentance. Now the exact language. Suppose you don't do that. Suppose you seek revenge for the hurt, even slightly in the tone of your voice or whatever? What then? The suffering you are going through "shall be accounted unto you as being meted out as a just measure unto you." What? The wrongs this person has done to me for forty years are going to be accounted a just judgment unless I've borne it patiently? That's what it says. Think of it.

It isn't an easy thing to do, but the commandment of the scriptures is that we are to forgive everyone—even those who are still hurting us. The opposite of it is to keep a laundry list of grievances and in the high pitch of an argument to bring them all up in serial form. That is not Christlike. Further, the person who will suffer the most is the person who does not forgive (see D&C 64:9). That is a law. So forgive. The person may or may not deserve it. Forgive anyway. How? Well, the scriptures give us one

clue. Jesus said, "Pray *for* your enemies" (3 Nephi 12:44). I have
italicized the *for*. It's easy enough to pray against, as in "Lord,
come down in judgment on this fiend and let there not be a
grease spot left." That's not praying for. That's seeking
vengeance. We must pray for, and the more we pray for, the more
we find ourselves feeling forgiving. And then a special blessing
comes to us. We accept that *we* are forgiven of the Lord.
Otherwise, we cannot be. I submit that it is psychologically impossible to really believe that you are forgiven of the living God if
you are still nurturing unforgiveness toward others. And that's
what the Lord's Prayer says. I am going to put it negatively, so it
will strike you. "Father, don't forgive me one inch more than I am
willing to forgive others." That's what it says. Forgive us as we
forgive others. If that's how much forgiveness we are going to receive, some of us are in trouble. As Joseph said, we haven't forgiven seventy times seven; perhaps we haven't even forgiven once
(see *Teachings*, p. 238).

Third point. President Kimball talks about selfishness.
Selfishness? What is that? Well, partly because of our culture,
partly because of human nature, we suppose that we are entitled
to more than we're getting. That's the real bottom line for a
Latter-day Saint. It isn't just that we are all frustrated—all of us
are. Perhaps no one in this world receives enough love. But it isn't
just that, it's that we feel in our heart of hearts that we are entitled
to more, and that hurts. Promises of the scriptures are constantly
before us: If you do this and this, then this will be the result.
Perhaps it doesn't seem to be working for us. Instead of getting
better, it is getting worse. So we say, "I'm entitled." President
Kimball's point is that we have to learn there is meaning even in
suffering; and we have to learn to care enough for blessedness that
we postpone some kinds of happiness. But isn't blessedness happiness? Of a sort, yes, but we learn by the example of Jesus Christ
that to bring about the happiness of others one must sometimes
go through lots of unpleasant experiences. And we aspire to be
Christlike. Well, is there a meaning in suffering?

A convert to the Church named Benjamin Crue was for a time
at the City of Hope Hospital in Duarte, California, as the head of
their chronic pain center. Fifteen different experts focused on one
patient each time—psychiatrists, surgeons, neurologists, pharmacol-
ogists, even people whose training was in physiological psychology.

Here were patients for whom no effort to reduce or remove pain had worked.

Benjamin Crue told me they learned something fundamental from their observations. They learned that when a person has chronic pain, unless he has at least one "significant other" in his life (a term used for someone about whom he cares and who cares about him), nothing we do really helps much with the pain. He told me this because of a sentence in my book that says love is the lasting therapy; a thing I believe, but had no evidence for. Now he gave me the evidence. He said that on the other hand, if there is such a person, even if it is only one—the person really cares about the sufferer and vice versa—then either he can cope with the pain or there can be substantial reduction in it. That's the power of love.

What is unbearable in life, I think, is the sense that what we are doing and suffering is meaningless—that there will be no adequate outcome from it, only more pain; that it all somehow is ended at death. But the gospel teaches us that, depending on us and our relationship with the Lord, even our worst struggles can be sanctifying, glorifying, and perfecting. It is a strange thing, is it not, that the same phenomenon—namely, pain—can have opposite effects, depending on one's attitudes and responses. For some it can lead to bitterness, the shriveling of the soul, hostility, and shaking the fist at God and all men; and to others it can lead to deeper love, deeper compassion, a more radiant exposure and expression, and eventually exaltation. Said Joseph Smith, "Men have to suffer that they may come upon Mount Zion and be exalted above the heavens" (*Teachings*, p. 323). Now, you may say, "Didn't Jesus Christ suffer so we wouldn't have to?" Yes, certain kinds of suffering He tempered or removed, including the suffering for sin. But once we take upon us His name our problems aren't all over. They are only beginning, for we are counseled to lose ourselves. And that's not selfish.

The question is frequently asked, Is marriage for procreation only? Answers come from the prophets. Let me read three. Joseph F. Smith speaking: "The relationship of man and wife is not only the sole means of race perpetuation, but for the development of the higher faculties and nobler traits of human nature, which the love-inspired companionship of a man and a woman can alone insure" (*Improvement Era* 20:739). Elsewhere the same prophet:

"Sexual union is lawful in wedlock, and if participated in with right intent is honorable and *sanctifying*" (*Gospel Doctrine* [Salt Lake City: Deseret Book Co., 1977], p. 309). Parley P. Pratt: "The union of the sexes is . . . also for mutual affection and cultivation of those eternal principles of never-ending charity and benevolence which are inspired by the Eternal Spirit; also for mutual comfort and assistance in this world of toil and sorrow and for mutual duties toward their offspring" (*Key to the Science of Theology* [Salt Lake City: Deseret Book Co., 1978], p. 105). The Doctrine and Covenants says of such a marriage as we are here describing, "It shall be visited with blessings and not cursings, and with my power, saith the Lord, and shall be without condemnation on earth and in heaven" (D&C 132:48). What a glorious truth! The giving of love by each partner in a marriage can itself be sanctifying to both the giver and the receiver. And what a glorious principle it is that ultimately we will be capacitated to give in fullness and receive in fullness!

That leads me to another glimpse beyond. The season of the dedication of the Kirtland Temple saw a great outpouring of the Spirit. In a Thursday fast meeting a man and a woman, apparently not husband and wife, stood up spontaneously, sang together a song in tongues, and then sat down; a song that they had never heard before so far as they knew, and words they did not fully understand. An interpretation was given by the gift of the Spirit. (See Edward W. Tullidge, *Women of Mormondom* [New York, 1877], pp. 208–9.) Think just for a moment of such a harmony of soul that two people who did not know each other until that situation, at least not in any depth, are literally transformed and are symphonically one. What a glimpse of possibilities!

Now, a few things about how love can find a way.

I had an uncle who had Parkinson's disease—he was in constant motion. His wife had arthritis and insomnia. When they climbed in bed at night he put his hand under her neck—a perfect vibrator—and slowly she relaxed and went to sleep. Then he pulled his hand over, and he went to sleep and the jiggle stopped. Love finds a way.

Many years ago President David O. McKay was being wheeled by President Tanner from his room in the hotel around to the elevators. When they reached the elevators he said, "Oh, I'm sorry, we must go back." President Tanner asked no questions and immediately pushed him back. What was the problem? He hadn't kissed Emma Ray good-bye. He was then ninety-three. Still some sizzle at ninety-three. Love finds a way.

Two other examples. In a ward I was in was a woman who had two children. Both were boys, and after age two both developed a rare disease in which every life process somehow reverses. I was asked to give a blessing to the second child, who had by that time lived to be twenty-one but was nothing but skin and bones—not even enough muscle left for lungs—and he shortly died. Because of the care her sons needed she hardly left that house, or even that room, for twenty-one years; and yet she and her husband were the most exciting youth leaders in the stake, had the most radiant kinds of personality, and were full of fun and games as well as wisdom. Love finds a way.

Years ago Elder Charles A. Callis went down to the southern states to organize the first stake there. With him was Elder Harold B. Lee, who also was a member of the Twelve. Elder Callis said of the first location that he could stay in a motel but would prefer to go back to a little old chapel-home where he and his wife had been accustomed to stay. This was one of those inseparable links after some fifty years, his wife having died. So he slept there while Brother Lee slept in a motel. The next day they came together. Traveling in a car, they had stopped and were waiting for a traffic light to change when Elder Callis turned and said, "Brother Lee, last night my wife came to me" and his head went down and he was gone from this life. Brother Lee organized the stake; then he gathered together Brother Callis's personal effects. And as he was walking out of that chapel-home he heard Brother Callis's voice say, "Well done, my boy." I heard Brother Lee say that the power of such love is what the gospel is all about. And he shook my lapels once when I was an aspiring young bishop, and said, "Brother Madsen, the most important work the Lord has given you to do is in the walls of your own home, and don't you forget it."

I recall a meeting at which Elder A. Theodore Tuttle was presiding. It was a big meeting—regional meeting, conference, priesthood meeting, I don't remember which. At about five minutes to nine, Elder Tuttle said: "Brethren, let's have closing prayer and adjourn. There are other things to consider, but let's adjourn, because one of you may have a date with your wife to go out and get

a malt, and nothing we can do here is more important than that."
The gospel teaches that the Church is the instrument to the glori-
fication of the family, not the other way around. And we all need
to keep that in mind.

It is a deep conviction of mine that the vision of eternal family
life that has been revealed through the Prophet Joseph Smith is
true. When President Kimball gave an address in which he talked
about how difficult marriage is—he spoke for sixty minutes on
how tough the drudgery and the diapers and the rest can be—he
tried to alert those young people who were thinking in terms of
"butterfly wings and honey" that once you get the woman off the
pedestal and on the budget, reality sets in. He warned them they
were wrong if they expected that just the initial *flash* of romance
and love would somehow perpetuate their marriage for the rest of
their lives. No, they were going to have to go and get more and
more of love, and then bring it home. And where do you get that?
In the temple, for one place, and by serving each other and receiving the Spirit; the more you increase in the Spirit, the more
you increase your power to love and be loved. Nevertheless,
having talked mainly in warning terms, even negative ones, about
the realities, he uttered this sublime, positive sentence: "Marriage
can be more an exultant ecstasy than the human mind can conceive" (*BYU Speeches of the Year*, 1976, p. 146).

Ecstasy is a strong word. I suspect most of us, in this world,
only taste it, but that is the word. The Lord promises us a fulness
of the glory of the Father, which is equivalent to the fulness of joy,
and that is worth giving everything for.

I have already mentioned that remarkable man Brother
LeGrand Richards. I wrote him because I didn't believe the story.
(It was subsequently published in his biography.) I now have a
letter which I will preserve to the end of my days. It tells of his
proposal to Ina, made after his first mission. He was walking along
with her, and everything was well between them, when he said,
"Ina, there is someone who will always come before you." She
gasped. She cried out, and she ran. She bolted, as women do to
cover the tears. When LeGrand caught up with her, he stopped
her and said: "Wait, wait, you don't understand. On my mission
there were times when the Lord was so close that I felt I could almost reach out and touch Him. He has to be the foundation of
our lives; but, Ina, if you want to be second, I want to marry

you." Now, I ask my female readers, is that an ideal proposal? Is that a highly romantic way to go about proposing to a girl? A girl said to me once, "I want a boy to say to me some day 'I love you so much I would go to *hell* for you.'" I couldn't resist saying, "What about going to heaven?"

The truth is that love should be triangular. If both partners, husband and wife, are really committed to the Lord Jesus Christ, then the love across the bottom of that triangle will flow powerfully. If either one of them or both is not, there will be problems. That's why the temple marriage is so different from eloping to Reno. The temple requires that you first make unconditional covenants with Christ, and then you can be trusted to kneel down and make unconditional covenants with each other. That is not required in Reno. Sometimes young people ask why, really what difference does it make? So much stress on going to that one building; why can't we go somewhere else? (By the way, President Lee taught that if you do have to go somewhere else, the second most sacred place on earth is . . .what? You don't go to the chapel or the reception center; you go to the home. That's the second most sacred place.)

Now, what I have testified over and over to young people is this: that it isn't *just* that when you go to the house of the Lord for your wedding certain things are said about forever; that's important, all-important, but that's talking about the *quantity* of the relationship. If it isn't of sufficient *quality*, however, there won't be that quantity. The temple ceremony is designed to give you the keys and powers of the transforming quality of love that will make that love worth perpetuating forever. You may say, "Just going through a ceremony surely doesn't do that." It does. I am troubled with people who disparage ceremony. The ceremony in this case is a channel, and all that precedes it—the whole temple ceremony, Elder Eldred G. Smith has said—is a temple *wedding* ceremony. Everything that precedes it and up through it is there to give to you divine powers, or at least to bestow them in the embryonic stage. And yes, returning and returning to the temple increases and increases those powers and one's understanding and perception of them. To deny these things is like saying you don't think that just taking an ordinary man and putting your hands on his head and saying a few words is going to make any difference in his life. The answer is, it does. There is a tangible mantle that goes with ordination and receiving the Holy Ghost and being called to positions of responsibility, and there is a tangible power from the Almighty God that is supposed to come to us through His temples to powerfully enrich our marriages. If you lack this conviction or feel that it has diminished, then I plead with you to do the things that will restore it and increase it. And if you say, "I don't love him or her anymore," then do the things that will cultivate love. They are clearly set out in the gospel of Jesus Christ.

The Lord who lives and loves is a Father and is not companionless. And His concern, His work and His glory, is that we should share in the fulness of eternal life that He enjoys.

9

ELIJAH AND THE
TURNING OF
HEARTS

There is something in the scriptures about an offering to be offered up one day by some specific persons, namely the sons of Levi. Puzzlement. Who are they? What is the offering?

In early 1847 Brigham Young was ill at a place called Winter Quarters. He had been prayerful and his feelings were mixed. He still was deeply grieved at the loss of his closest earthly friend, Joseph Smith, and was burdened heavily with the kingdom and its leadership. He was puzzled over the question of adoption. Some of the Saints whose own literal forebears showed a lack of interest or even deep hostility regarding the Church wished they could be grafted into a faithful family. Some such ordinances were performed. Now Brother Brigham was praying about it.

He had a dream in which he saw the Prophet Joseph Smith. Some beautiful passages demonstrate that Brother Brigham wanted to join the Prophet. If you think that wasn't sincere and lasting, you should know that his last words on earth, thirty years later, would be one word three times repeated—"Joseph, Joseph, Joseph."

After this 1847 interchange and the assurance the Prophet there gave him that he must live on, Brigham inquired about adoption and the Prophet replied. In the account there are seven different ways in which he says, "Tell the people to get and keep the Spirit of the Lord."

There is a marvelous statement about how we know the spirit received is the Spirit of the Lord, for Joseph says at one point, "They can tell the Spirit of the Lord from all other spirits; it will whisper peace and joy to their souls; it will take malice, hatred, strife and all evil from their hearts; and their whole desire will be to do good, bring forth righteousness and build up the kingdom of God." Then the interesting conclusion: "Be sure to tell the people to keep the Spirit of the Lord; and if they will they will find themselves just as they were organized by our Father in Heaven before they came into the world. Our Father in Heaven organized the human family [in the premortal councils], but they are all disorganized and in great confusion." (*Manuscript History of Brigham Young, 1846–1847,* February 23, 1847.) So much for Brigham Young's glimpse of the crucial nature of the Spirit in finding ourselves united in a family relationship.

But now to the scriptures for a moment. It could be said that the earliest and latest revelations in the Doctrine and Covenants touch on this theme, the first being section two (which was actually given before section one). That is the revelation or statement of Moroni to the Prophet Joseph Smith in 1823. It says that Elijah will be sent. And what for? To "plant in the hearts of the children the promises made to the fathers, and the hearts of the children shall turn to their fathers" (Joseph Smith—History 1:39). Elijah will be among those who participate in the most glorious family reunion in all history. It could be called a sacramental wedding breakfast to be held following the Lord's second coming. (See D&C 27:5–14.)

Elijah did come. He came to the Kirtland Temple on April 3, 1836. (See D&C 110:13–16.) Jewish literature is replete with the promise and expectation of Elijah's coming. That is the last promise of the Old Testament, in the last verses of Malachi. And it is Jewish tradition that on the second night of Passover they must leave open the door and place at the table head an empty chair and a goblet full of wine in the expectation that Elijah may come. It is interesting, especially in light of that Jewish tradition, that April 3, 1836, was the second day of Passover. The symbolism is beautiful. Elijah comes, as they expect, to a home. He comes to a goblet of wine—the sacramental wine. He comes to turn hearts, which is more than changing minds—he turns hearts to hearts.

He somehow bridges some gap, some alienation, some separation that has occurred in the human family.

No subject preoccupied the Prophet Joseph Smith more than this one. In his later years he spoke at least eight times pleading with the Saints to ponder and pray over this principle. We ordinarily say that Elijah did something pertaining to the dead or work for the dead. A half truth. In the first place, no one is really dead. Those who are in the spirit world are, as we are taught by the prophets, more alive than some of us here. Elder Melvin J. Ballard used to say that they have "every feeling intensified" spiritually. And as for their being dead and gone, no, they are not gone either. The prophets teach us that the spirit world is not in some remote galaxy; it is here, it is near. And as the Prophet put it, speaking of their feelings for us, those who are bound to us somehow by the anxieties of their forebearing, "their bowels yearn over us" (*Teachings,* p. 159). He said they "are not idle spectators" in the last days (*Teachings,* p. 232). He explained, "Enveloped in flaming fire, they are not far from us, and know and understand our thoughts, feelings, and motions [one account says emotions], and are often pained therewith" (*Teachings,* p. 326). And he could have added, "rejoiced therewith." When the scriptures say, "All eternity is pained," that is, I take it, a metaphor for the pain of these spirits. Similarly when they say, "the heavens weep for joy."

So Elijah does have something to do with them. But the Prophet taught that he also has something to do with us, with the living. Had he not come, the whole earth would be cursed; or in another version, the earth would be utterly wasted at Christ's coming. Wasted, I take it, means at least two things. It would be in a sense a waste if this earth, created by our Father and His Son as the dwelling place of their family, turned out to be a house barren. Not a home. Not a place of genuine familial love. In that sense it would have been a waste to create it. But second, were there not a family welded and united and full of love for Christ, it would be the case that all mankind, unable to endure His presence, would be laid waste at His coming. Thank God for the restoration of the power to prepare such a family. That conferral came through Elijah.

The Prophet said, speaking of this, "How shall God come to

the rescue of this generation?" And he answered, "He will send Elijah." (*Teachings,* p. 323.)

Well, that generation may have been a difficult one, but this generation in which you and I live is in some ways a worse one. Constantly students ask me around the country, "Do you think the world is getting better or worse?" And I always answer, "Yes." The wheat is getting "wheatier" and the tares are getting "tarier"— and rapidly.

How can a mere prophet change a whole generation, and an ancient prophet at that? Well, we can know a few things about him. Know that his name is interesting—El-i-yah: literally, in Hebrew, "My God is Jehovah." But more than that, it symbolizes the sealing or the union of father and son. Know that he conferred keys, and we understand, if only dimly, that means authority— priesthood authority. There are men on the earth today who hold those keys by direct line of ordination. Every marriage in this Church that is binding both here and hereafter has been performed under those keys and their delegated authorities. Second, Elijah had a revelatory function. There is a spirit that is somehow emanating through him and his work and ministry which has reached out far beyond the bounds of this Church, turning hearts and not just heads. And one account says that it was his function to reveal to us "the covenants of the fathers in relation to the children, and the covenants of the children in relation to the fathers"—perhaps pointing to something that happened prior to mortality. Elijah is also an exemplar of what is his mission, for it is not yet over. As a translated being, one not yet subject to death, he had the unique privilege of ministering to the Master and the three Apostles on the Mount of Transfiguration (see Matthew 17:1–8) in an experience which we are told we cannot yet fully understand, the fulness of the account having been reserved for the future. A Jewish apocalyptic tradition says that those two prophets who are to one day testify in the streets of Jerusalem to prepare the hearts of the Jews to be turned to the prophets (see D&C 98:16–17), and are then to literally be killed and lie in the streets—martyrs just prior to the coming of the Messiah—are Elijah and Enoch. Elijah has been patient through millennia awaiting the opportunity to bring earth and heaven back together, to tie together the old and new worlds, to take the estranged and the alienated and the embittered and somehow transform their hearts, and to prepare all of the family who will to be family, welding them indissolubly in order to greet the Christ.

Let us draw a few personal and emotional implications from this. Feeling, after all, centers in the heart, and the role here is not one of mere intellect. It is a matter of feeling something inside. The Prophet said on one occasion to the Relief Society that he grieved that they were not exhibiting greater union of feeling among them. And he went on to say, "By union of feeling we obtain power with God" (*History of the Church* 5:23). When he introduced the ordinance of the washing of feet in Kirtland among the brethren, he taught them that this ordinance—an essential one—was to enhance the union of feeling and affection among them, that their faith might be strong (see *History of the Church* 2:309). And repeatedly the Lord has said in modern revelation that He reveals himself by His Spirit to the mind and the heart. "Behold, I will tell you in your mind and in your heart by the Holy Ghost which shall come upon you and which shall dwell in your heart" (D&C 8:2), an impressive blending of intellect and sentiment.

Now, we need not dwell on the point that in our culture the family is coming unglued. There are those who hold that the great wave of the future, a better future as they see it, is to totally abandon the notion of united families—and they recommend it. One can call attention to devastating statistics outside the Church, but I want to talk strictly about inside it. One of our statistics, and I am only approximating, is that there are well over 600,000 children in this Church who are being raised by a single parent. There are delinquent fathers. There are delinquent children. Just from conversation in my own office over the years on the BYU campus I have heard sentences that tell it all. For example, "My mother gave me five hundred dollars and told me to go away." Or: "I couldn't possibly tell my father. He would kill me." Or again, "My mother has been divorced three times." Or again, "No one in my family cares anything for the Church." Or again, "Just before I left for my mission my father threatened to take my life." Or again, "I don't dare go home."

Robert Frost saw it clearly on the home. He said, "Home is where, when you get there, they have to take you in." Would that it were so. Many who are joining the Church in this generation are doing so at the cost of never being permitted through that door of home again. My own great-grandfather wrote a letter from Nauvoo. He was a squire—a kind of amateur attorney—who had loved the Mormon people but had never joined them. And his motivation was elementary: he had a wife and a son, and both of them said that if he ever did, that would be the end; they would never speak to him again. The letter to Brigham Young says, "Is this what the Lord requires of me?" And Brigham Young's answer, in a word, was "yes." My great-grandfather joined the Church, and his wife and his son kept their word.

Yes, we are in a real world. And the alienation, the pain, the hostility, the torment, the trauma, even in some Latter-day Saint homes, is a long distance from Elijah, who said he would turn hearts toward and not away. Is there hope? There is.

Let's discuss now not what one needs to do but what one needs to feel. First there is forgiveness. We are glib, I think, in quoting the passages that talk about our needing to forgive, and even to forgive all people. They are there. One of the strongest passages is in the context of the Prophet Joseph and his own weaknesses, his pleading with his brethren to forgive him, pleading as the revelation does; and then going on to say that if they don't, there remaineth in them the greater sin (see D&C 64:9). Strong language, saying that one's refusal to forgive a sinner is a worse sin than whatever sin the sinner has committed. Well, forgiveness is the very nature of Christ's way. I suggest that it may be difficult to forgive your enemies, but it is even more so to forgive your loved ones who have sometimes manifested hate—and you have too, in response. It is harder to forgive your loved ones because you care about them and you have to go on living with them, or struggling to, and they can go on hurting you over the years and the decades. But our hearts will never turn to our fathers in the way this spirit of which we have been testifying motivates us to do unless we forgive.

You see, we have inherited all kinds of things. There is a standard procedure for students with bad report cards. They can go home and say: "Look, Mom," or "Look, Dad." "Which do you think it is, heredity or environment?" And their parents can say, "Neither of the above." The fact is that we willingly chose to come into the world, likely in this time and circumstance. And when a young person says to his parents in deepest animosity, "I didn't ask to be born," if they give the proper, prophetic answer

they will say: "Oh yes, you did. You not only asked for it, you prepared for it, trained for it, were reserved for it." I am saying that
both he and they are mutually involved.

And by the way, that's a snarl word in our generation.
Involved. No one wants to get involved, in anything. Do your own
thing. Be yourself. But you and I and all of us are involved. It was
collusion. And therefore, as you look back at the seventy or so
forebears—and that's what it would take at fifty years each, only
seventy to get you back to Abraham—you might recognize that
you have inherited the blood of generations And *blood* may be
not a correct word scientifically, but it stands in the scriptures for
seed, which is specifically the heredity, the inheritance of tenden-
cies, and all of us have them. And so you have the blood of this
generation, from which we must become clean—"clean from the
blood of this generation" (D&C 88:85). If you are, you will be
clean from the blood of every generation, because it is com-
pounded and accumulated into now. And that includes the blood
of some degeneration.

So perhaps you do have problems that you can blame on an-
cestors, and if you forgive that and choose to stand close to the
Lord in the process of purifying your life, that will affect your
whole family in both directions. You are not alone. There is no
way you can regain solitary and neutral ground. You are in it—in
involvement. And this, I take it, is one of the profound meanings
of that long, laborious allegory in the book of Jacob, the allegory
of the tame and wild olive trees. If you take a wild branch and
graft it in to a tame one, if the branch is strong enough it will
eventually corrupt and spoil the tree all the way to the roots. But
if you take a tame branch and graft it in to a wild tree, in due time,
if that branch is strong enough, it will heal and regenerate to the
very roots. You will then have been an instrument in the sanctification even of your forebears.

Do these considerations ever sober us in moments when we
suppose either that no one cares for us or that whether they care
or not, our life makes no difference? To be that kind of branch
and achieve that kind of transformation backward and forward is
perhaps the greatest achievement of this world. But to do it one
must be great, one must be linked, bound to the Lord Jesus
Christ. One must be mighty. One must be something of a savior.
And that is exactly what the Prophet Joseph Smith said we are—

"saviors on Mount Zion" (*Teachings,* p. 330). And how are we to be saviors on Mount Zion? he asked once in a discourse. He answered by saying that we do so by (first building then) going into the temples of the Lord, and in our own first person presence, going through all the temple ordinances for and in behalf of loved ones who have passed on. This can "redeem them that they . . . may be exalted to thrones of glory." And it will help "fulfill the mission of Elijah." (*Teachings,* p. 330.) Yes, saviors, redeemers of our families.

We have many examples in our history. I chose this one not because it is exceptional but because it isn't. Erastus Snow, given a blessing by the Prophet Joseph Smith, was told in effect: "Brother Erastus, your father knows nothing of the gospel of Jesus Christ, but the Lord God will be your Father and He will watch over you. And if you will walk in the full path of righteousness, the time will come when you will save all of your kindred flesh; and in due time, if you are worthy, these blessings which I pronounce upon you will be confirmed upon you by your own father. And then your joy will be full."

The capacity to forgive comes only through the capacity for loving the Lord Jesus Christ. And He taught us how. He said, "Pray for your enemies." That's different, I remind you, than praying against your enemies. If you want to know how you can turn feelings of hostility into feelings of forgiveness and love, that's the how. You pray for them. You may choke in the effort, but as you keep going, the time comes when you mean it. And then you not only mean that you want to forgive, and feel it, but you even find yourself praying that He will forgive. And you look with compassion instead of spite at the whole traditional mix that has made you what you are and to some degree what you aren't. So much for forgiveness.

Now, the other is even harder. The word is *sacrifice.* And we know that the family of man was taught from Adam down to make external sacrifice with the firstlings, the firstborn. These were consumed, burned on an altar, all to typify and prepare for the coming of the living sacrifice, who was Christ himself. We now know that when the Lord appeared to the Nephites He said, in substance: "No longer will I accept burnt offerings. From now on I will accept only your hearts. You must bring to me the sacrifice of a broken heart and a contrite spirit." (See 3 Nephi 9:19–20.)

We use the term "broken heart" to mean radically frustrated in a romance. That meaning is accepted, but in the scriptural usage a broken heart is a malleable, meltable, moveable heart, and a contrite spirit is an honest, acknowledging spirit that says, "I am, in fact, dependent on what I am in fact dependent on." There is not self-deprecation here, only honesty: "I need help." And when that is acknowledged, help comes.

I suggest that one sacrifice the sons of Levi and the daughters of Levi are to offer in the end is the willingness to give themselves in the cause of saviorhood and to care more about family and the preservation and intensification of family than they care about anything else in this world. That has costs. Some things have to be given up. Some things have to be postponed. And the focus is sacrifice. I have to say honestly, I believe it is painful. I have to say I believe that there are many among us who are easily pulled in other directions. And I have to say I consider that a tragedy. I occasionally hear housewives say that they are "mere housewives." What have you done in the last twenty years? Oh, nothing—just fed my family three meals a day and more or less kept them together. Is that all? President Lorenzo Snow said with power on one occasion that if a woman raised a righteous family she would be exalted in the celestial kingdom (cited by Leroy C. Snow in a Snow family reunion program). Our generation is making attractive every other thing but. That is not the gospel of Jesus Christ.

So I plead with you, be forgiving and be sacrificial.

Flying in from the Far East some time ago, I found on the plane a young man obviously recognizable as a Mormon Elder. We chatted. I didn't at first tell him who I was or that I really already did think the Mormon church was great. But I soon learned that there were three things a little unusual about him. First, his father had died while he was on his mission. When I was myself a mission president, I prayed every night and every morning for two things. One, that I would not have to send any missionary—male or female—home in disgrace. And two, that I would not have to send an Elder or a Sister home dead. In a way that's an unfair prayer, because I suspect that, with tens of thousands of young people out in the real world, in the long run there is no way to avoid some lapsings. But I so prayed. I had not foreseen another difficulty, and that was to have to call in a missionary and tell him that one or the other of his parents—or in one case both—were gone.

Well, this Elder on the plane had lost his father. His father had not been particularly faithful in the Church. His mother had taken up the burden, and of course, as required, had sent the monthly check. The second thing was that he had let his mother know he was coming home, but he hadn't told her when. And the third thing was that he hoped to go to BYU. As I got off the plane, and I was first off, I saw a face and something told me that this was his mother. I restrained myself from telling her that her son was on the plane. I went to a position where I could see both her face and his. He got off and walked along a bit casually, carrying cameras and briefcase. And then he saw her. There was recognition, gratitude, forgiveness for whatever may have been amiss in the past, and a total royal embrace. That's it. That's everything.

It is precisely that kind of embrace and reunion which you and I were sent into the world to make possible with loved ones in a future existence. It will not be possible except we are repentant and have faith in the Lord Jesus Christ sufficient to enable us to forgive and to sacrifice. That is our mission and our commission.

Occasionally when I have been in Jerusalem I have tried to picture in my weakness what He promises us will happen there one day. Mount Olivet, or the Mount of Olives, is the place from which He ascended. It is the place of His greatest suffering. It is the place where there was a garden, *Gat shemen;* in Hebrew, Garden of Oil Press, where, as it were, He trod the olive press to produce the oil of healing, the balm, the peace. That place today, if you study it carefully, is a place of everything except reunion. It is a place of destruction. Graves are everywhere. Shattered things are everywhere. Barbed wire, glass, the droppings of animals, everything you can name. And hostility and bitterness is symbolized on that very mount in the fact that different faiths, each with its own claim, build churches, build basilicas, and then each refuses to acknowledge the existence of the other. There are machine gun remnants. There is a monument to a place where paratroopers in the Six-Day War were gunned down by the dozens. War is what is symbolized there.

Yet the promise of the Lord Jesus Christ is that He will descend to that mount (see D&C 45:48). His foot will touch it. It will then cleave in twain, and there will be an earthquake. Dramatic, but true—an earthquake covering the whole earth. And there will be a transformation of the earth, preparing it for its terrestrial condition. As He descends with His worthy hosts, the privilege will also be given to those who remain here to be caught up together to meet Him. We will not have to simply remain and wait, but as in every genuine effect of true love, we will want to take our own steps toward the full embrace.

Thus it is our privilege and calling to become in our own limited way redemptors of the human family, ours and His. It is impossible to love Him truly and not love what is His; and God assigned Him all of us. And it is not possible for us to really love ourselves unless we love what is truly us, and that is the whole house of Israel in which we belong. As we learn to do this and accordingly act as saviors, we will be helping to fulfill the great mission of Elijah.

10

HOUSE OF
GLORY

I begin with a story that goes back to the dedication of the Salt Lake Temple, which took forty years to build. President David O. McKay used to tell of a man who didn't have money enough even to buy shoes to attend a conference in the Tabernacle. During the conference Brigham Young arose and pleaded with the brethren that there needed to be more granite brought for the temple from the quarry about fifteen miles south. It was hauled mostly by ox team. A man came out from this conference and saw another man on the street with a team of oxen. "Why weren't you in there, Brother?"

"Uh, my feet. I didn't feel right about going in."

"Well, Brother Brigham pleaded for more people to get granite."

"All right," said the man, "I'll go. Wo hah, Buck!" And he started.

President McKay's eyes filled with tears as he related that simple incident. The reason why his name and his image come to mind whenever I think of temples is that it was President McKay who performed the wedding ceremony for my wife, Ann, and myself, and that high privilege was possible for us in part because he had done the same for Ann's parents. That morning, very early on a June day, he came in his white suit, a white tie, and white hair. There was majesty in his personality. Somehow we knew then, had

we ever doubted it, that no one could speak properly if he spoke
evil of the temple, for there before us stood its product.

John the Revelator, John the Beloved, visioning the city
Jerusalem in glorified state, said "And I saw no temple therein: for
the Lord God Almighty and the Lamb are the temple of it"
(Revelation 21:22). And then he added that not only would the
Lamb reign forever, as we sing, but we, having by then been glori-
fied like unto Him, would likewise reign forever and ever (see
Revelation 22:5).

The Salt Lake Temple was dedicated with a sense of sacrifice
and gratitude that maybe we moderns have not reached. Forty
years! Forty thousand people gathered just to see the laying of the
capstone! And Lorenzo Snow, then one of the Twelve, led them
in the Hosanna Shout. And then Wilford Woodruff, who had had
a dream years before that he would somehow be involved in the
dedication of that temple (and he was by now the President of the
Church), promised that a strict reading of the requirements of
worthiness would not be imposed on the members attending the
dedicatory services provided they come feasting and repenting.
(That was not a slip of the lip, because the Lord defines fasting
and prayer in modern revelation—granting it has its negative side
of mourning in some places—as rejoicing and prayer (see D&C
59:13–14). Fasting is feasting on the Spirit, and somehow not
partaking of physical food isn't quite enough. Fasting is a kind of
concentration, a kind of pulling ourselves together.)

Well, during a twenty-three-day period of dedicatory services
averaging two thousand each session, some eighty thousand people
were regenerated. President Woodruff's entry in his journal at the
end of that year was: "The greatest event of the year [1893] is the
dedication of the Salt Lake Temple. Great power was manifest on
that occasion." (Matthias Cowley, *Wilford Woodruff* [Salt Lake
City: Bookcraft, 1964], p. 584.)

The scriptural phrase that brings all that into a theme is that
we are to receive in temples, through temples, from temples,
"power from on high" (D&C 95:8). Christ is the source of that
power. The temple is His. Every symbol in and out of that sacred
structure points toward Him and, as a cup carries water, transmits
the Holy Spirit.

Now to be specific in terms of needs that all of us feel strongly
about in our time. It is a characteristic fact that the Lord has com-

manded the sacrifice of temple building at the times when apparently our people were least able to build them; and the sacrifice has been immense. But sacrifice "brings forth blessings."

In the 1830s the Brethren kept inquiring. They didn't have our heritage, and they didn't understand even what the word *temple* meant. They kept asking, What is it we are doing? Well, we build a temple. What for? And Joseph Smith told them on one occasion, "nor could Gabriel explain it to [your] understanding." But prepare, he told them, for great blessings will come. (See *Teachings,* p. 91.)

Yet in a preparatory revelation (see D&C 88) the purposes of the temple are outlined. It's called "a house of prayer, a house of fasting, a house of faith, a house of learning, a house of glory, . . . a house of God." Prepare yourselves, it says, "sanctify yourselves . . . and [God] . . . will unveil his face unto you." (D&C 88:68, 119.)

Let's discuss each of those purposes.

A house of prayer. "Make yourselves acquainted," said the Prophet, "with those men who like Daniel pray three times a day toward the House of the Lord" (*Teachings,* p. 161). There is a true principle involved in literally facing the house of God as one prays and as one praises the Lord. The Prophet, as he led a group of faithful Saints through the Nauvoo Temple not yet finished (he did not live to see that day), said to them, "You do not know how to pray to have your prayers answered." But, as the sister who recorded that brief statement testifies, she and her husband received their temple blessings, and then came to understand what he meant. (See *They Knew the Prophet,* p. 123.)

A modern Apostle, Elder Melvin J. Ballard, said once to a group of young people about solving their problems: "Study it out in your own minds, reach a conclusion, and then go to the Lord with it and he will give you an answer by that inward burning, and if you don't get your answer I will tell you where to go; go to the House of the Lord. Go with your hearts full of desire to do your duty. When in the sacred walls of these buildings, where you are entitled to the Spirit of the Lord, and in the silent moments, the answer will come." (*Utah Genealogical and Historical Magazine,* October 1932, p. 147.)

For clues to personal experiences behind that statement we note that in Elder Ballard's boyhood he often looked up at the

Logan Temple and its spires, was inspired by those spires, and wanted to enter the temple worthily regardless of the costs. That meant, for one thing, that he never was even tempted to break the Word of Wisdom, because he knew that might prevent him from entering that building. His later experiences, many having to do with his ministry, were a derivative often of what he felt, experienced, tasted within the walls of the sanctuary.

On a personal note, I myself, in a critical year away from home and at school, drove at times to the place in Los Angeles where we had been told there would one day be a temple, just in the feeling that the place might be an added strength to me in prayer. And it proved to be so.

"A house of prayer, a house of fasting, a house of faith, a house of learning." One of the men who touched my life was Elder John A. Widtsoe of the Council of the Twelve, a man who graduated summa cum laude from Harvard after three instead of the usual four years, who was given in that last year an award for the greatest depth of specializing in his field (which was chemistry); but they also gave an award that year for the student who had shown the greatest breadth of interests, which he also received. Elder Widtsoe wrote perceptively about the temple and temple worship. I heard him say in sacred circumstances that the promise was given him by a patriarch when he was a mere boy in Norway, "Thou shalt have great faith in the ordinances of the Lord's House." And so he did. I heard him say that the temple is so freighted with depth of understanding, so loaded with symbolic grasp of life and its eternal significance, that only a fool would attempt in mere prosaic restatement to give it in a comprehensive way.

I heard him say that the temple is a place of revelation. And he did not divorce that concept from the recognition that the problems we have are very practical, very realistic, down-to-earth problems. He often said, "I would rather take my practical problems to the house of the Lord than anywhere else." In his book *In a Sunlit Land* he describes a day when, having been frustrated for months in trying to pull together a mass of data he had compiled to come up with a formula, he took his companion, his wife, to the Logan Temple to forget his failure. And in one of the rooms of that structure there came, in light, the very answer he had previously failed to find. Two books on agrarian chemistry grew out of that single insight—a revelation in the temple of God.

The temple is not just a union of heaven and earth. It is the key to our mastery of the earth. It is the Lord's graduate course in subduing the earth, which, as only Latter-day Saints understand, ultimately will be heaven—this earth glorified.

A house of learning? Yes, and we learn more than about the earth. We learn *ourselves.* We come to comprehend more deeply, in an environment that surrounds one like a cloak, our own identity, something of the roots that we can't quite reach through memory but which nevertheless are built cumulatively into our deepest selves—an infinite memory of conditions that predate memory. The temple is the catalyst whereby the self is revealed to the self.

There was a period when I was required as an officer in the Ensign Stake to go every Friday to the temple. It was not a burden, as I had thought it would be. It became instead my joy. Slowly, because of that regularity, I was trusted with certain assignments in the temple. This meant that I could walk into the temple annex and they would all say, "Good morning, Brother Madsen"; and I wouldn't even have to show my recommend. Not only that, but I had the privilege to sit for hours in the chapel of the annex or elsewhere, contemplative, reading occasionally, but trying to absorb, trying to breathe the air that is heavier than air in that place. There I would meditate about my critical problems, which had to do with decisions about my life's work, decisions about the girl I should marry, and other struggles in how to cope. There were times when I learned something about me; there were times when peace came in a decision, and I knew that that peace was of God.

The temple is a house of learning. And it is intended that therein we not simply learn *of* or *about* Christ, but that we come to *know Him.* It has always impressed me that in the Joseph Smith Translation the classic passage about the hereafter when many will say, "Lord, Lord, did we not do this and that?" is rendered more fittingly. The King James Version says that Christ will respond, "I never knew you." The Joseph Smith Translation renders it, "You never knew me." (Matthew 7:23; JST Matthew 7:33.)

This is the gospel of Jesus Christ. This is the restored Church of Jesus Christ. This is the church that teaches us that we can have a direct and immediate living relationship with the living Christ. And we inscribe on temples, "Holiness to the Lord," "The House of the Lord." He told us, and He didn't qualify it, that as regards our preparation, "all the pure in heart that come into it shall see God" (D&C 97:16). Elder Orson Pratt points out that this promise specifically relates to a temple not yet built, a temple to be erected in the center city, the New Jerusalem, wherein someday Christ actually will dwell; and wherein, therefore, any who enter will meet Him. But again, Elders John A. Widtsoe, George F. Richards, Joseph Fielding Smith, and others have borne witness that the promise is more extensive than that; that it applies now. It is a promise that we may have a wonderfully rich *communion* with Him. *Communion!* That is to say that we are not simply learning propositions *about,* but that we are in a participative awareness *with.*

Occasionally we struggle in amateur research in Church history to understand what kind of a portrait, in terms of sheer physical appearance, one could draw of Christ if we simply utilized what modern witnesses have said about their glimpses of Him. It's an impressive portrait. But one thing perhaps we sometimes neglect in that curiosity is an awareness or a seeking for an awareness of His personality, of those subtler realities that we already recognize in other persons in all variations but which have been perfected in Him. What would it be like to be in His presence, not simply in terms of what you would see but what you would feel? To give us one clue, He says, "Listen to him . . . who is pleading your cause before [the Father], saying: Father, behold the sufferings and death of him who did no sin [that is to say, committed none, but he knows sins, for he experienced temptation to do them all], in whom thou wast well pleased; behold the blood of thy Son which was shed, . . . wherefore, Father, spare these my brethren." (D&C 45:3–5.) That's a glimpse of the compassion that one comes to feel in communion—the feeling with, the feeling for, that He has. He is the one personality of whom it cannot truthfully be said: "You don't know me. You don't understand me. You don't care about me." Because of what He went through, He does know, He does understand, He does care. And He has had us sacrifice to build sacred houses where the linkage of His heart, His "bowels of compassion," can merge with ours.

The temple is a place of learning to know Him.

And now the phrase "a house of glory, a house of God." One of the most tender moments of my spiritual life was the day that Rose Wallace Bennett, an author I knew, told me that as a little girl she was present in the dedicatory services of the Salt Lake Temple. She described also the day Wilford Woodruff had a birthday, his ninetieth, when it was a little girl's privilege to take forward to him in the Tabernacle ninety roses in a setting of some eight thousand children between the ages of eight and twelve, all dressed in white. They had gathered to honor him; and then as he had come into the building (under some pretense that there was need of an organ repair), they arose and sang, "We Thank Thee, O God, for a Prophet." She could not talk about what it felt like to see his tears, or again, what it was like to be in the temple, without herself weeping. But what she said to me was: "Young man, my father brought me to the edge of City Creek Canyon where we could look down on the temple. I testify to you that there was a light around the temple, and it was not due to electricity."

There are such phrases in all the authentic literature that has to do with temple dedications: "light," "glory," "power." Even some who were not members of the Church at Kirtland came running, wondering what had happened. They wondered if the building was on fire. It was; but with what the Prophet called "celestial burnings," the downflow of the power of the living God, like encircling flame as on the day of Pentecost. A prayer for that had been offered by the Prophet and by his father, and it was fulfilled. (See D&C 109:36–37); *History of the Church* 2:428; *Women of Mormondom,* p. 101.)

What is glory? Well, it is many things in the scriptures. One strand of meaning is often neglected. If we can trust one Hebrew student, the Hebrew word equivalent to glory, *kabod,* refers in some of its strands to physical presence. Just as a person says in common parlance today, "he was there in all his glory," so the Old Testament often uses this word for God. In the Psalm that refers to the glory (Psalm 8) there are two changes that are crucial. The King James Version reads, "Thou hast made [man] a little lower than the angels, and hast crowned him with glory and honour." Probably what that verse said originally was, "Thou hast made [man] a little lower than the Gods, and hath crowned him with a *physical body* and with honor." This is the truth. The body is a step *up* in the scales of progression, not a step down. God is God because He is gloriously embodied; and were He not so embodied, He would be less than God.

The privilege of attending the house of God is in effect to have our physical beings brought into harmony with our spirit personalities. And I have read, but cannot quote perfectly, can only paraphrase, the testimony of President Lorenzo Snow to the effect that participating in the temple ceremonies is the only way that the knowledge locked in one's spirit can become part of this flesh; thus occurs that inseparable union, that blending, which makes possible a celestial resurrection. It is as if, if I may mix the figure, we are given in the house of God a patriarchal blessing to every organ and attribute and power of our being, a blessing that is to be fulfilled in this world and the next, keys and insights that can enable us to live a godly life in a very worldly world, protected—yes, even insulated—from the poisons and distortions that are everywhere.

That is the temple. And the glory of God, His ultimate perfection, is in His house duplicated in us, provided we go there with a susceptible attitude.

Let me briefly discuss the "how" of susceptibility. Listening once in Los Angeles to the plea of President David O. McKay, stake president after stake president pledged contributions to make possible the building of the Los Angeles Temple. They made a commitment. Then he arose and delivered a masterful discourse, maybe the greatest I have ever heard on the subject of temples. In shorthand I jotted down one paragraph which I'm going to quote, but before I do so, let me give this explanation. He told of a girl—a girl, I found later, who was his niece and therefore felt confident in confiding in him. Earlier that year she had been initiated in a sorority, and not long thereafter she had "gone through the temple" (as we say); I wish that verb could be improved—"going through the temple." I wish we could somehow speak of the temple going through *us*. I wish that my children had not been confused—it's my fault that they were—when my wife and I used to say to them, "We are going to *do* sealings." They thought that we would take a stepladder and a bucket. It's a kind of Mormon activism to talk about "temple work." There is a sense, of course, in which it is work; but too rarely do we speak of "temple worship," which can send us back to our work changed.

Well, on the occasion in Los Angeles, President McKay stopped everyone by saying: "This young lady came to me. She had had both experiences, but said she had been far more impressed with her sorority." We gasped.

President McKay was a master of the pause. He let that wait for several seconds and then said: "Brothers and sisters, she was disappointed in the temple. Brothers and sisters, I was disappointed in the temple." Then he finished his sentence: "And so were you." Then no one gasped. He had us.

"*Why* were we?" he asked. And then he named some of the things. We were not prepared. How could we be, fully? We had stereotypes in our minds, faulty expectations. We were unable to distinguish the symbol from the symbolized. We were not worthy enough. We were too inclined quickly to respond negatively, critically. And we had not yet seasoned spiritually. Those are my words, but they cover approximately what he said. I will give you the quotation verbatim.

This was a man, at that time eighty years of age, who had been in the temple every week for some fifty years, which gave him, I thought, some right to speak. He said: "I believe there are few, even temple workers, who comprehend the full meaning and power of the temple endowment. Seen for what it is, it is the step-by-step ascent into the Eternal Presence. If our young people could but glimpse it, it would be the most powerful spiritual motivation of their lives."

When he said that, I felt it. I had myself been a critic; had made up my mind that some things were trivial, offensive. But that day the Lord touched me, and I decided that I would not speak again against the house of the Lord. I would not assume I knew better than the prophets. I would listen And I would repent. And I would hope that someday I could testify as did that noble man. In time there was far more opened up to me than I had ever dreamed.

But there were three things amiss in me, and I dare to suppose these may apply to some others. First, I hadn't even carefully read the scriptures about the temple. It had not occurred to me that there are over three hundred verses, by my count, in the Doctrine and Covenants alone that talk about the temple and the "hows," if you will, of preparation. I had not read what the Brethren had said to help us—I was unaware of those statements. Today we are well supplied with informative material in books such as *The House of the Lord,* by Elder James E. Talmage; *The Holy Temple,* by Elder Boyd K. Packer; and several articles in the *Encyclopedia of Mormonism,* volume 4.

Second, I was, I am afraid, afflicted with various kinds of unworthiness and not too anxious to change all that. Oh, we talk of it and we aspire. We want change, but we don't want it enough. We are (and I don't laugh at poor Augustine for saying this) like Augustine, who said in a prayer, "Oh God, make me clean, but not yet." We talk of sacrifice. The one the Lord asks of *us now* is the sacrifice of our sins—the hardest thing in the world to give up. There's still a certain bittersweet enjoyment. But His promise is crystal clear. "If you will purify yourselves, sanctify yourselves, I will bless you" (see D&C 88:74). And I'm afraid the postscript is: "And if you don't, I can't."

The third point is that I had a built-in hostility to ritual and to symbolism. I was taught by people both in and out of the Church—with good intention, I have no doubt—that we don't believe in pagan ceremony; we don't believe in all these procedures and routines; that's what they did in the ancient apostate church: we've outgrown all that. Well, that in effect is throwing out the baby with the bath water. We're not against ordinances. God has revealed them anew. And I suspect they are as eternal as are what we often call eternal laws. There are certain patterns or programs, certain chains of transmission, which are eternal. Ordinances tie in with those, if they are not identical with them. God has so decreed, but that decree is based upon the very ultimate nature of reality. You *cannot* receive the powers of godliness, says the scripture, except through the ordinances (see D&C 84:20). Well, that hadn't ever entered my soul. I thought our sacraments were a bit of an embarrassment and that sometime we could do away with them. One day it suddenly became clear to me—this is the Lord's pattern of our nourishment. We need spiritual transformation. We can eat, if you will, receive, drink (the Lord uses all those images) the Living Fountain through ordinances.

Well, I pray that we will reach out for what is written, reach out for repentance, and reach out in the recognition that the ordinances are channels of living power.

The dedicatory prayers for temples have from the beginning been given by revelation, and that fact has been puzzling to some. How can the Lord reveal a prayer to offer to Him who has revealed it? Well, there's nothing contradictory in that. One cannot know fully what to pray until he receives guidance from the Lord. "He that asketh in the Spirit," says modern revelation, "asketh according to the will of God" (D&C 46:30). You must listen in order to know what to say. And prayers that are all ask and no listen lack something in effectiveness.

The temple is the place where we can come to understand what the Lord would have us ask. And it is the place where we can ask in silence, in joy, in earnestness.

Years ago I was involved in the Ensign Stake Genealogical Committee. We held a series of firesides. The climactic one of six was given by President Joseph Fielding Smith. The last lecture was given on temple marriage. But the week before that I had been asked to speak on vital temple purposes. I struggled with that. I was talking to young people. What was most remarkable came toward the end of what I said. I wanted somehow to let them know that my own assurance about marriage had come within the walls of the temple.

But I didn't want to acknowledge publicly that I was going to marry this girl. That had not yet been said in private, and therefore I didn't think it should be said in public. But there came down on me that night (and I have a tape-recording that tells the story) such a witness that I announced, "The Lord has made known to me that I am to be married, and to whom." She was on the front row, sitting next to my father. It came as a bit of a surprise to him, too. There was much salt water spilled. Have you heard Pasternak's phrase, "Be so close to those you love that when they weep you taste salt"? I did. I gasped, though, at what I had said and wanted somehow to alter, qualify, call back, change. That was shown in several seconds of silence. Then at last all I could do was say, "In the name of the Lord, amen," and sit down.

For all of us there is something about the temple that can change our lives. We need to reach for it, to honor it, if need be to sacrifice for it, even our sins. Some of us have fought against that, as I fought against it, because it means change, maybe some painful change. But that change is the Spirit of God working on the soul and it will come to each one of us. We will honor the promptings and let the Lord take over in our lives.

The Lord *is* in His temples, where He ministers personally and manifests himself to the faithful therein. With the power of Christ in His sanctuary, it is intended that all of us drink deeply, receive powerfully, and then testify worthily of that glorious truth. In this way we will come to share in the joys and blessings of the radiant life.

INDEX